THE EASTERN SCHISM

THE EASTERN SCHISM

A STUDY OF THE
PAPACY AND THE EASTERN CHURCHES
DURING THE
XITH AND XIITH CENTURIES

BY

STEVEN RUNCIMAN

OXFORD
AT THE CLARENDON PRESS

Oxford University Press, Great Clarendon Street, Oxford OX2 6DP
Oxford New York
Athens Auckland Bangkok Bogota Bombay
Buenos Aires Calcutta Cape Town Dar es Salaam
Delhi Florence Hong Kong Istanbul Karachi
Kuala Lumpur Madras Madrid Melbourne
Mexico City Nairobi Paris Singapore
Taipei Tokyo Toronto Warsaw
and associated companies in
Berlin Ibadan

Oxford is a trade mark of Oxford University Press

Published in the United States by
Oxford University Press Inc., New York

First published by Oxford University Press 1955
Reprinted 1956
Special edition for Sandpiper Books Ltd., 1997

British Library Cataloguing in Publication Data
Data available

ISBN 0-19-826417-8

3 5 7 9 10 8 6 4

Printed in Great Britain by
Bookcraft Ltd
Midsomer Norton, Somerset

PREFACE

THIS book is based on seven Waynflete lectures given in the University of Oxford in the Hilary term of 1954 at the invitation of the President and Fellows of Magdalen College. I am deeply grateful for the honour of that invitation and for the opportunity with which I have thus been provided for a discussion of one of the most controversial and unhappy chapters in the history of Christendom.

A full and detailed account of the division between the great Churches of the East and the West could only be covered in a work of many volumes. The pages that follow are intended to offer a brief presentation of those facts which I believe to be essential for the understanding of the story. The history of the controversy has usually been left to the pens of theologians, not without reason; for the battlefield on which Church leaders challenge each other is one of doctrine and of religious usage. But wars are not started on the battlefield; and, just as it would be unwise to employ soldiers alone to write the history of a war and its causes, so it is useful to regard a schism from a viewpoint that is not purely theological. It is my aim to show that the Eastern Schism was not fundamentally caused by differing opinions on the Procession of the Holy Ghost or the Bread of the Sacrament but by the conjunction of political events and the prejudice and bitterness that they aroused with a growing divergence in basic ideology, which the political events forced on to the notice of the world.

It used to be generally held that, after the solution of earlier quarrels between the great Patriarchates, schism was started anew in a more dangerous form by Photius, Patriarch of Constantinople, and that though the division that he caused was patched up after his death it broke out again in a final and irrevocable form owing to the Patriarch

Michael Cerularius. The writings of Professor Dvornik and Father Grumel have taught us that the traditional view of Photius must be greatly modified; and scholars are now reaching the conclusion that the year 1054, the date of the breach between Michael Cerularius and Cardinal Humbert, can no longer be held to mark the final separation of their Churches. The separation came more slowly and more unevenly, when the Norman invasion of Italy, the greater invasions of the Crusaders, and the vigorous actions and ideas of the reformed Papacy gradually forced on to the notice of Eastern Christendom the extent to which the Eastern and Western point of view on the Universal Church had moved apart.

I am deeply in debt to the distinguished scholars whose works have helped to clarify the history of the Schism. It was M. Jules Gay whose history of Byzantine Italy was the first book to put the events of 1054 in a clearer perspective. The publications of Professor Michel and of the Catholic ecclesiastical historians Amann, Jugie, and Leib, as well as the Anglican writer George Every, have further enlarged our understanding of the whole episode. The references in my footnotes will show how much I owe to them in detail, but I should like to acknowledge herewith my larger obligations to them.

It is difficult to treat of a controversial subject without rousing disagreement and resentment. But I hope that none of my words will cause offence to followers of either the great Church of Rome or the Churches of the East. If my personal sympathies incline towards Byzantium, it is because I have tried to understand the Byzantine point of view. Most of the writers who have dealt with the unhappy question have belonged to the Latin world; and though nothing could be more scrupulously fair-minded than the writings of such Catholic scholars as Father Jugie or Father Amann, the full Byzantine case has often been allowed to go by default. It is my belief that only by a fuller understanding of each other's feelings and traditions can the Churches be brought into closer friendship; and though I do not think it possible that terms can now be found on which the breach can be healed, it is my hope that this book will in no way embitter the problem but may help a little to lessen ill will.

S. R.

London 1955

CONTENTS

I

THE HISTORICAL BACKGROUND

IT is an article of faith that the followers of Christ should form one united body on earth. The Creed put forward by the Fathers at Nicaea as well as the shorter Apostles' Creed ordains belief in the Holy Catholic Church; and all good Christians must wish that the high ideal of an undivided Church could be realized. But human nature is not uniform, nor is human religious experience. Complete agreement on ecclesiastical theory or practice among the diverse peoples of the Christian world has never been achieved. 'I hear that there be divisions among you', wrote Saint Paul to the Corinthians;[1] and the example of the Church of Corinth has been copied perpetually down the ages.

The usual definition of a schism is that it is the emergence of a separate faction within the Church, whereas heresy is associated with false doctrine. This seems to be the sense in which Saint Paul uses the two expressions. According to Saint Augustine, schism is a broken fellowship of communion, but does not affect the Faith or the Sacraments. The Early Fathers frequently blurred the distinction between schism and heresy; but it came to be generally accepted that while the latter represents doctrinal error, the former represents Orthodox dissent.[2] Strictly speaking, the great Churches of the East and the West, which for convenience we usually call the Orthodox and Catholic Churches, should regard each other as heretics. The Orthodox consider that the Catholics have

[1] I Corinthians xi. 18.

[2] St. Augustine of Hippo, *De Fide et Symbolo*, 21, *M.P.L.*, vol. xl, col. 193. See Greenslade, *Schism in the Early Church*, pp. 19–20.

tampered wrongly with the Creed ordained by the Holy Oecumenical Councils to be the common symbol of Christendom, while the Catholics have raised their theory of Church authority, which the Orthodox reject, to be an article of faith. But in fact, though Orthodox theologians have in the past tended to exaggerate theological differences and Catholic theologians cannot condone what they consider to be a wanton repudiation of the rights of the See of Saint Peter, the division still essentially concerns the question of authority rather than that of doctrine and is therefore more in the nature of a schism.

It is possible to analyse the causes of schism under five headings. It may be due to personal rivalries; to nationalistic, social, or economic rivalries; to the rivalry of the great sees; to liturgical disputes; or to problems of discipline.[1] In the story of the quarrel between Eastern and Western Christendom personal rivalry in the narrow sense was absent. The protagonists fought as representatives of their sees, not as individual claimants for the same see. The character of each of them naturally affected his attitude towards the dispute and his tactics; and on occasions personal dislike exacerbated the dispute. But the rivalry was essentially between the sees. This rivalry was, however, largely an expression of nationalistic rivalries and itself raised problems of discipline. Nationalistic pride also made liturgical disputes more bitter, while liturgical differences were largely due to temperamental divergencies, themselves partly the result of social and economic trends; and a long sequence of political events embittered and distorted the quarrel.

When a schism concerns a single Church, we can fix with some precision the moment when it began. When it concerns the greatest Churches of the time, it is less easy to say when the absolute breach occurred. The official symbol of unity was provided by the diptychs, the lists

[1] Greenslade, op. cit., pp. 19–20.

kept by each Patriarch in the churches of his see for the commemoration of the Patriarchs, past and present, with whom he was in communion. When a new Pope or Patriarch was elected it was his duty to send round to his fellow Patriarchs his declaration of faith; and thereupon, unless the declaration was rejected as heterodox, his name was added to the diptychs. It might seem, therefore, that if a Patriarch's name were omitted from the diptychs of another see, that see and his were in schism. But in fact that deduction was only valid if there were constant means of communications between the sees. After the breakdown of the Roman Empire there were times when a newly elected Patriarch was quite unable to send his Systatic Letter, which was his declaration of faith, to his fellows. If they failed to commemorate him it might often be through sheer ignorance of his existence.[1] After the Arab conquests of the seventh century there were long periods during which the Oriental Patriarchs were completely out of touch with Rome and even with Constantinople, and there were huge gaps in their diptychs. Moreover, particularly in the East, there were Patriarchs whose election seemed to be uncanonical or whose theology seemed to be dubious, and whose names were therefore omitted till further information arrived; but this was not thought to impugn the orthodoxy of their sees. Omission from the diptychs did not necessarily involve a schism.

It is more accurate to date the schism from the moment when rival lines of Patriarchs, Greek and Latin, appeared to contest each of the great sees. There must be some sort of schism in existence for this to happen. But it happened at a different date in each Patriarchate. But a state of schism may well exist before there is a conflict over a particular bishopric, while on the other hand such a conflict does not

[1] For the significance of the diptychs see Every, *The Byzantine Patriarchate*, p. 31, and Langford-James, *A Dictionary of the Eastern Orthodox Church*, p. 46.

of necessity mean that the various elements within that particular bishopric consider themselves to be separated one from another.

In fact, the state of schism only came into being when the average member of each Church felt it to be there; and that feeling developed slowly over a period of years and cannot be attached to any single date.

Fundamentally there had always been a difference in outlook between the Eastern and Western halves of the Christian world. Eastern Christendom grew up in countries imbued with the Hellenistic spirit. Its cultural background and its common language was Greek; and it inherited the old Greek delight in speculative thought. The Eastern provinces of the Roman Empire were far better educated than the Western; and the Church there developed in an atmosphere where everyone, layman and priest alike, was interested in theological discussion. Long before the Triumph of the Cross under Constantine, many of the best intellects in the East had adopted Christianity; but the attempt of each thinker to extract in his own way the full philosophical significance of the Christian Revelation produced endless debates and disputes. It became a delightful pastime to prove that opponents had lapsed into heresy, that is to say, that their philosophical deductions had perverted the Christian Revelation. Nobody was going to accept as orthodox the views held by any one theologian without full argument. It was therefore felt that the correct faith could only be ascertained by a general assembly at which all the members of the Church were represented. Such an Oecumenical Council was the successor of the meeting of the Apostles at Pentecost; and it was hoped and believed that, as at Pentecost, the Holy Ghost would descend and inspire the discussions, so that the truth would prevail. The system had its disadvantages. The assemblies were often stormy. Physical violence was not unknown. It was sometimes difficult to be sure that the Holy Ghost had really been present. The minority was seldom willing to accept the ruling of the majority; and if its dissent was enhanced by some wider grievance, such as the nationalistic and economic grievances of the Syrians and the Egyptians in the fifth century, then the dissidents might lapse into permanent heresy. But that was a slow process. The Council of Chalcedon, whose findings were rejected by most of the congregations in Syria and Egypt, took place in 451. But it was not till the time of the Arab conquests, nearly two centuries later, that the Copts and the Syrian Monophysites were held to be hopelessly heterodox. Till that time there had always been a hope that an Oecumenical Council might be inspired to find a formula that would smooth over the difference. Moreover, the Eastern Church, accustomed as it has always been to divergencies, has always believed in a principle that is called Economy; which means quite the opposite to economy in the modern sense, but, instead, the distribution of alms or charity or dispensation. The exercise of a little charity enables a good Christian to overlook discrepancies, so long as there is an atmosphere of mutual goodwill. The principle of Economy, and its limitations, must be kept in mind when we study the story of the dispute with Rome.[1]

When the Emperor accepted Christianity he was accepted as the head of the Christian community. Constantine, for his services to the Church, was raised to the rank of Equal to the Apostles. As Church and State came together, it was held to be the Emperor's business to see to the well-being of both. It was for the Emperor to summon an Oecumenical Council and to preside over it, in person or by proxy. His coronation became before long a religious ceremony and gave a religious backing to his authority; but that authority was based on the fact that he was Emperor, the heir to the Caesars. The great hierarchs of the Church

[1] The principle of Economy (οἰκονομία) is discussed in Langford-James, op. cit., pp. 47–50.

were definitely inferior to him. His position was recognized even in the West. When the Popes later claimed rights from the forged Donation of Constantine, the strength of their claim lay in the belief that the Emperor had made the donation. Though the Patriarchs were nominally elected by their bishops, the Emperor in fact appointed them and deposed them, more or less at his will.[1] This Caesaropapism must not be exaggerated, even as regards Byzantium. Official law-books stated that the Emperor and the Patriarch were together the chief organs of the body politic and harmony between them must be preserved, though the Emperor was the senior partner.[2] It was generally felt that an Emperor should not interfere in ecclesiastical affairs except through the Church; and if a matter of doctrine was concerned, a council must be called. A Patriarch who had the moral backing of public opinion behind him could effectively oppose the Emperor and could go so far as to refuse to perform a ceremony of coronation.[3] The strength of the Church lay in its moral influence; and an Emperor who flouted that did so at his peril. His subjects would be justified in staging a revolution. But, though he could not afford to outrage moral susceptibilities, the Emperor had one supreme asset. He was the source of law. The Roman Empire lasted in the East till 1453, and its law was Roman law. Successive codes showed increasing Christian influence, but they were all issued by the Emperor. The Church's interest in law was limited to purely ecclesiastical matters.

[1] See Bury, *Selected Essays*, pp. 113–18 ('The Constitution of the Later Roman Empire').

[2] Bury, *History of the Later Roman Empire from Arcadius to Irene*, ii, p. 415, citing Leo III's *Ecloga*; Basil I, *Epanagoge*, iii. 7, in Zachariae von Lingenthal, *Collectio Librorum Juris Graeco-Romani ineditorum*, p. 68.

[3] In 491 the Patriarch Euphemius refused to crown Anastasius I, whose orthodoxy was suspect, till he gave a satisfactory statement of his faith. Bury, *Later Roman Empire*, i, p. 431. In 969 the Patriarch Polyeuct refused to crown John Tzimisces till he abandoned his adulterous connexion with the Empress Theophano. Cedrenus, *Synopsis Historiarum*, ii, pp. 380–1.

Even over such questions as marriage and divorce the rules of the Imperial code were obeyed. The ecclesiastics were therefore for the most part uninterested in law and without legal training. The lawyers were laymen with a layman's outlook.

Nor were the lawyers the only educated laymen. Throughout the history of the Eastern Empire there was a large lay population that was as well educated as the clergy. The professors, the government servants, and even the soldiers were usually as cultured as the priests. Many of them were highly trained in theology, and almost all of them felt themselves perfectly competent to take part in theological discussions.[1] No one in Byzantium thought that theology was the exclusive concern of the clergy. The part played by the laity is exemplified by the fact that it has never ceased to be the practice to administer communion in both kinds to the lay members of the Eastern Church.

It was probable that because there were in Byzantium so many passionate theologians, amateur as well as professional, there was a tendency to avoid a definite pronouncement on many questions of belief. The Orthodox view was not always clear. Byzantine theologians when supporting the same side in a dispute often put forward arguments quite inconsistent with each other's. When heresy-hunts were instituted, the cause was either because the heresy was socially undesirable, as, for instance, Bogomilism, or because the hunt provided the means for suppressing some party or person who was unpopular or dangerous. Where there was goodwill charity prevailed.

Right worship was really more important to the East Christians than right belief. They were devoted to their liturgy, though it did not become definitely fixed till after the Iconoclastic controversy. But that very controversy had

[1] Many of the most learned Patriarchs, such as Nicephorus and Photius, were laymen until their appointment to the Patriarchate. See below, p. 23.

shown that their attachment to their forms was growing. The liturgy was something in which the whole congregation played its part; and even the decoration of the church building was involved in it; the icons and mosaic figures, too, were participants. They grew to resent very bitterly any criticism of their ritual and their practices, and were suspicious of attempts at innovation or alteration. They admitted that the liturgy might be translated into vernacular languages for the use of alien Churches, and, rather grudgingly, that certain other forms of the liturgy were sufficiently hallowed by time and tradition to be permissible. But their loyalty to their own liturgy was probably the strongest single spiritual force in the make-up of the Byzantines. It inspired their best art and their best poetry and music; and the humbler members of the Empire felt an even stronger loyalty to it than the educated.[1]

The whole attitude of the medieval West was different. Christianity spread more slowly in the West than in the East, and paganism lasted on much longer there, particularly in cultivated circles. The Church there was obliged, for its self-defence, to insist on the need for unity and uniformity of belief. At the same time there was less general interest in speculative philosophy and less desire, therefore, for theological debate. Language played its part in the difference. While Greek is a subtle and flexible tongue, admirably suited to express every shade of abstract thought, Latin is far more rigid and inelastic; it is clear, concrete, and uncompromising, a perfect medium for lawyers. Political circumstances soon harnessed the legalistic quality of Latin civilization to the service of the Church. When the Imperial authority broke down in the West, under the stress of barbarian invasions, the only organization that survived was the Church. The Imperial viceroys and governors vanished; but the Pope and the bishops remained. They were the leaders who negotiated with the barbarian

[1] See Every, op. cit., pp. 27–31.

conquerors, and who continued to administer the cities. When the new secular states settled down on a permanent territorial basis their laws for the most part were customary and tribal. The written law, with the prestige of the Roman Empire behind it, was preserved by the Church. Where tribal law was insufficient, the Church filled up the gaps and thus enlarged its sphere of legal influence. Prominent ecclesiastics had to become lawyers themselves. Thus, while in the surviving Empire in the East the Emperor remained autocrat and the source of law, in the West his authority, though it was not officially rejected for centuries, was in fact ineffective; and his place was naturally taken by the head of the Church, the Bishop of Rome, who gradually inherited his position as autocrat and the source of law.

Even in Roman times the level of culture had been generally lower in the Western provinces than in the Eastern; and the barbarian invasions had a very destructive effect on secular education in the West. The cultured lay circles of Italy were extinguished during the wars and troubles of the fifth and sixth centuries. The only education that survived was conducted by the Church for the Church. In the early Middle Ages there were few laymen in the West who could even read. This gave the Church in the West a position in society that the Eastern Churches never possessed, until the distant date when the secular Christian authority there was ended by conquest by the infidel. Unlike the Eastern Liturgy, the Western Mass was a mystery performed by the priesthood, and the lay congregation did not have the same intimate feeling of participation. Moreover, while the language of the Byzantine Liturgy was roughly intelligible to the average Byzantine, the Latin of the Mass was a foreign language to most of the faithful in the West. The Western laity was seldom permitted to interfere in any matter of religion. On the other hand, the clergy, who were the intellectual *élite*, continually interfered in the affairs of State.

The autocratic constitution of the Western Church under the Pope was the inevitable product of historical forces. It received its theoretical justification from the Petrine claims. Saint Peter had been the Prince of the Apostles, the rock on which the Church was built, endowed with the keys of Heaven and the power to bind and loose. He had died as Bishop of Rome; and his successors in the bishopric which he had founded inherited his powers. The Pope was not only supreme governor of the Church but also supreme arbiter on doctrine. An Oecumenical Council, if properly constituted, would indeed be inspired by the Holy Spirit; but its function was to endorse and promulgate papal pronouncements. Faith became a series of articles embodying divine laws. Certain doctrines were right and lawful; others were wrong and unlawful. Religious speculation was not to be encouraged; it was centrifugal and dangerous. Moreover, from his position the Pope was identified with his Church. An insult to the Pope was an insult to the whole Western Church. No Eastern Patriarch personified his Church to such an extent. If he were insulted, the insult was usually held to apply to his person alone. An Eastern Patriarch remained always a man who might be fallible and even heretical. Only the Church of the Councils was infallible. In the West infallibility was an implicit prerogative of the Pope.

The Western Church thus tended to become a centralized body under an autocratic and divinely inspired head, a body directed by experienced administrators and lawyers, whose theology reflected their outlook. Many centuries elapsed before this tendency was fully realized in the Papacy of Gregory VII and Innocent III; but it was always there, and had it not been there the Church of Rome could hardly have survived the troubles of the Dark Ages.

It is not surprising that as the centuries passed Eastern and Western Christendom found it increasingly difficult to understand the other's point of view. They both shared the same fundamental belief in Christ Jesus and in the Holy Trinity and in the Sacraments. But their practices diverged even over the administration of the Sacrament, and their rituals were entirely different. The outlook of each of them to theology was essentially alien to the other. The East enjoyed speculation and argument; but the official Church was ready to exercise charity towards unessential divergencies, and avoided doctrinal pronouncements and condemnations except when political issues or the liturgy was involved. The West had a simpler, stricter, and more legalistic and logical conception of right and wrong belief. In the East there were large numbers of educated laymen and laywomen accustomed to play a part in religious affairs, and there was an articulate public opinion that did not hesitate to criticize both the Emperor and the hierarchy. Neither an educated laity nor a public opinion that was articulate on religious matters existed in the West before about the twelfth century; and even then its criticism was directed against the behaviour, not against the beliefs, of the clergy. Almost from the outset East and West held incompatible views about ecclesiastical authority. The Later Roman Empire, the Empire of Byzantium, had no room in its constitution for claims such as the Pope's. The Emperor, the heir of Constantine, Peer of the Apostles, was responsible there for the administration of Christendom, while doctrine was the concern of an Oecumenical Council. In the West the Pope was heir to the Emperor as well as to Saint Peter. The Donation of Constantine, which was later produced to justify papal authority, was a forgery; but most of what Constantine was therein said to have given to Pope Sylvester was in fact inevitably acquired by the Popes in the course of history.

The division between the Churches was enhanced by the difference in language. If more of the Greeks had understood Latin and more of the Latins Greek, their Churches might have found the other's point of view more comprehensible. In many of their disputes harm was done by an unintentional error in translation.[1] Understanding does not necessarily create sympathy, but at least it provides a basis for the use of tact and forbearance. Tact and forbearance are at the best of times qualities that are unusual in ecclesiastical circles; and when their absence is exaggerated by ignorance, the results are disastrous. If the great Churches of East and West had never been brought into close contact with each other, peace might have been preserved by mutual indifference. But contact was inevitable, and it inevitably provoked enmity, made more bitter by the fact that both Churches were genuinely and sincerely Christian and both believed that the Church of Christ, the Holy Catholic Church, should be one and universal.

At the time of the Triumph of the Cross under Constantine the Church was divided into three great Patriarchates, Rome, Alexandria, and Antioch, arranged in that order of precedence. The Romans later claimed that Rome came first because her Church had been founded by Saint Peter. But Alexandria was considered by the Romans themselves to come before Antioch; yet the Antiochene Church had been founded by Saint Peter and the Alexandrian only by Saint Mark. It could not therefore be said that precedence depended upon the apostolic foundation. Rome's pre-eminence was basically due to the city's position as the Imperial capital; and Alexandria came next because she was the second city of the Empire, the equal in size and wealth to Rome itself. But Rome had a special prestige, not only because the Empire was the Roman Empire but also because Saint Peter and Saint Paul had both culminated their careers there. The Roman bishop therefore enjoyed

[1] Baynes, *The Byzantine Empire*, p. 95; Jugie, *Le Schisme byzantin*, pp. 39–42. Much of the trouble in the Photian dispute was due to mistranslations and the misunderstanding of established formulae. Pope Nicholas I took offence at being addressed as Bishop of 'Old Rome', though that was the honorific Byzantine name for his see. Dvornik, *The Photian Schism*, pp. 104–5.

particular respect and was generally expected to give a lead in ecclesiastical affairs. His leadership was rather more than a purely honorary primacy, but it was not clearly defined nor legally constituted.[1] There was, however, after the official recognition of Christianity a tendency by the Emperors to establish the constitution of the Church along legal lines; and had Constantine and his family not lapsed towards Arianism, a doctrine denounced by the Roman See, it is possible that the Bishop of Rome might have become the official head of the Church organization. The Council of Sardica, which in 343 made Rome the court of appeal for ecclesiastical disputes, pointed in that direction.[2] But already the situation had been complicated by the foundation of Constantinople, the New and Christian Rome which was designed to take over the role of Imperial capital. The Bishop of Byzantium had hitherto been of little importance, a mere suffragan to the Archbishop of Heraclea; but the Bishop of New Rome must clearly enjoy a more splendid rank. He was soon raised to be a Patriarch, and his Patriarchate was given a wide territorial jurisdiction at the expense of Rome and of Antioch. The division of the Empire broke down the notion that there was only one administrative centre; and the Church was still inclined to copy the organization of the secular State. The Second Oecumenical Council, which met at Constantinople in 381 to finish off the Arian controversy, declared in its third canon that 'the Bishop of Constantinople shall rank next to the Bishop of Rome, because Constantinople is New Rome'. The Fathers who passed the canon had no intention of thereby humiliating Old Rome. They

[1] Jugie, op. cit., pp. 57–100, gives numerous examples from the fourth century onwards of admissions by Oriental churchmen of the primacy of Rome. But I think that he tries to draw too exact a legal meaning from these admissions, and at the same time does not draw a sharp enough line between primacy and supremacy.

[2] The relevant canons (Nos. 3 and 5) are given in Hefele–Leclercq, *Histoire des Conciles*, ii. 1, pp. 762–6, 769–77.

were merely paying a realistic compliment to the new capital, with the additional aim of lowering the pride of the Patriarchate of Alexandria, whose great bishop Athanasius had become embarrassingly influential. But the Emperor Theodosius, who had summoned the council, did not summon the bishops whose sees were in the territory of his Western colleague, Gratian. The Pope was therefore not represented and could officially refuse to recognize the canon. The Fourth Oecumenical Council, the Council of Chalcedon, at which the Pope was represented, endorsed the rights of the See of Constantinople in its twenty-eighth canon, saying that the Fathers had correctly assigned the precedence to Old Rome because it was the Imperial city and that 'equal privileges should be given to the most holy throne of New Rome', because 'the city which is honoured with the sovereignty and the Senate and enjoys equal privileges with the old Imperial Rome should be magnified as she is in ecclesiastical matters and rank next after her'. The Eastern Churches supported this canon, which was carried by a majority; but the papal representatives opposed it and the Pope rejected it. Indeed its wording was not quite fair to the claims of Rome, for it took no account of the tradition of the apostolic succession from Saint Peter, which was of considerable if unspecified importance, nor of the special leadership in Church affairs that the many eminent bishops of Rome had taken. Indeed, the Byzantines themselves were a little uncomfortable about it. Even in times of bitter controversy they always were anxious to declare their respect to the See of Saint Peter; and their not very convincing attempt to prove that the Church of Constantinople had been founded by Saint Andrew showed that an apostolic foundation was now held to be of value. Further, the wording of the canon was not sufficiently clear. It did not define what were the privileges enjoyed by Old Rome; nor had they anywhere been defined. Was Constantinople, for instance, to share with Rome the right to hear appeals, which the Council of Sardica had given to the older city? It was not surprising that the Pope protested against the canon.[1]

The Council of Chalcedon also raised the See of Jerusalem to patriarchal rank. Rome again protested, but along different lines. Jerusalem was undeniably the Holy City, where Christ had taught. Its Church had been founded by Saint James, the brother of Our Lord; and Saint James, as the Scriptures showed, had been regarded as the head of the whole Church. So the Roman argument was that on the one hand the apostolic Church there had been ended when Titus destroyed the city and on the other Jerusalem was now no longer sufficiently important as a town to enjoy such advancement. In the end Rome recognized the Patriarchate of Jerusalem.[2] There was, in fact, no accepted rule in such matters. The East was already prepared to consider an Oecumenical Council as the inspired authority in all matters of doctrine and organization, while the West considered that the only ultimate authority was the successor of Saint Peter.

These divergent views became more clearly apparent during the great Christological controversies that tormented the Church from the fourth to the seventh century. They ended with the secession of the chief Christian congregations in Syria and Egypt, and with Rome and Constantinople in full but uneasy communion with each other. During the course of the dispute Rome gave definite expression to her point of view. At the time of the Council of Chalcedon Pope Leo I declared categorically that the true

[1] Hefele–Leclercq, op. cit. ii. 2, pp. 24–27 (3rd Canon of Constantinople, and commentary), pp. 815–18 (28th Canon of Chalcedon), pp. 840–1 (the Pope's rejection of the canon). A reply by the Patriarch Anatolius (ibid., p. 855) seems to imply that he would abandon the canon unless it was approved by Rome. But in fact the Eastern Churches accepted its validity.

[2] Hefele–Leclercq, op. cit. ii. 2, pp. 735, 740. See Vailhé, 'L'Érection du Patriarche de Jérusalem en 451', in *Revue de l'Orient chrétien*, vol. iv (1896), pp. 44–57.

faith was embodied in his own statement, the so-called *tomus*. The Eastern Churches were not prepared to agree to this. But the tact of the Imperial authorities secured that the *tomus* should be the basis of discussion at the council and should be accepted as correct, after a few additions had been made to elucidate certain points.[1] Unfortunately the findings of Chalcedon were rejected by most of the Christians of Syria and Egypt, who lapsed into Monophysitism; and any Emperor who sought to evolve a compromise that would reconcile his Monophysite subjects was faced by the stern refusal of Rome to modify the *tomus*. The Patriarch of Constantinople was almost always obliged, from his proximity to the Emperor, to whom he owed his appointment, to follow the Imperial lead; and thus the good relations between Rome and Constantinople were continually interrupted. When the Emperor Zeno promulgated his *Henoticon*, which was a vain attempt to satisfy everybody, he was supported by the Patriarch of Constantinople, Acacius. Pope Simplicius thereupon excommunicated Acacius, and his successor, Pope Felix III, declared him deposed.[2] This led to a breach between the Churches of Rome and Constantinople, which lasted from 484 to 518, though peace was nearly made in 498, when Pope Anastasius II showed himself ready to make a compromise; for which his own Church called him a heretic and Dante was later to place him in Hell.[3] In 518 the Emperor Justin I, who was eager for political reasons to secure the friendship of Rome, obliged the Patriarch John II to erase Acacius and his four successors from the official diptychs and to concur in the formula that 'the Catholic Faith was kept inviolate by the Apostolic See'.[4]

[1] The *tomus* or *Epistola Dogmatica* of Pope Leo is given in Hefele–Leclercq, op. cit. ii. 2, pp. 567–80. It was addressed to Flavian of Antioch.

[2] Hefele–Leclercq, op. cit. ii. 2, pp. 865–8, and notes.

[3] Duchesne, *L'Église au sixième siècle*, pp. 113–28; *Liber Pontificalis*, ed. Duchesne, i, p. 258; Dante, *Inferno*, ix. 8–9.

[4] The correspondence between Justin I and Rome is given in the *Collectio Avellana*, letters 141–81, ed. Gunther, ii, pp. 586–638.

During the reign of Justinian I the Popes were roughly treated by the Emperor, but they did not lose ground against the Patriarch of Constantinople. The same is true of the events of the seventh century. The Monothelete controversy ended at the Sixth Oecumenical Council with the Roman view triumphant over the views held from time to time by Emperor and Patriarch. But, while four Patriarchs of Constantinople were officially denounced as heretics, one Pope, Honorius I, was included in the list of heretics, though the Latin translation of the acts of the council tactfully omitted his title of Pope; and two Patriarchs who had definitely not been in communion with Rome were admitted to have been orthodox.[1] Rome did not come quite unscathed out of the conflict; and everyone knew that the truth had prevailed less from papal action than from the energy of a Greek ecclesiastic, Maximus the Confessor. Moreover, the victory of Roman theology was largely due to Imperial intervention. The Emperors considered the Pope to be their subject as well as the Patriarch; and the Pope was more important because he was physically less easy to control and politically more useful owing to the influence that he commanded in Italy. Thus if the Pope could only be placated by humiliating the Patriarch, the Emperor was usually prepared to order the Patriarch to recognize papal superiority, and was himself anxious to show deference to the Pope's office. When the Emperor Phocas, who reached the throne after peculiarly nauseating bloodshed, was sent a fulsome letter of congratulation by Pope Gregory I, who should have known better, he replied fulsomely, acknowledging the Pope as head of the Church.[2] When Pope Constantine I visited Constantinople, the Emperor Justinian II greeted him by kneeling crowned before him. His gesture was rewarded by the Pope's acceptance, with a qualifying formula, of the canons of the

[1] Hefele–Leclercq, op. cit. iii. 1, pp. 511–12.

[2] Gregory I, *Epistolae*, xiii. 31, *M.P.L.*, vol. lxxvii, coll. 1281–2.

Council *in Trullo*, which hitherto Rome had deliberately ignored.[1] It must, however, be remembered that while the Popes, from the nature of their claims, could never admit that they had erred, the Eastern Church did not consider that its hierarchs were infallible. A Patriarch's expression of opinion was not binding on his successors; nor was an Emperor's, unless it was embodied in a law. Even the canons of an Oecumenical Council, binding though they were, could be improved or clarified. The East had no thought of creating strict legal precedents in religious matters in the manner of the West. Thus if some eleven Patriarchs of Constantinople admitted the superiority of the Pope, they made the admission at the Emperor's bidding, and their successors felt themselves at liberty to consider them wrong in so doing.

The only apparent act of aggression made by the Patriarch of Constantinople was the adoption of the title of Oecumenical Patriarch by John the Faster in 595. This title roused the fury of Pope Gregory I, who took it to mean that the Patriarch claimed world-wide jurisdiction and who induced the Emperor Phocas to forbid its use. But in fact it meant less than the Pope supposed. To the Byzantines the Oecumene, though it literally implied the whole inhabited world, was used to connote the Christian Empire. Constantinople was the Oecumenical capital; and its Patriarch was therefore the Oecumenical Patriarch. It was an honorific epithet, which certainly did not give him any authority over his fellow Patriarchs, any more than the Oecumenical Professor at the University, the Professor of Philosophy, had authority over the other Faculties.[2]

The secession of the Nestorian and Monophysite communities in Syria and Egypt was crystallized by the Arab con-

[1] Hefele–Leclercq, op. cit. iii. 1, pp. 578–80.

[2] See Jugie, op. cit., pp. 22–24. The Council of Chalcedon had offered the title to Pope Leo I, who had refused it (Hefele–Leclercq, op. cit. ii. 2, pp. 834–5).

quest. It was in the Moslems' interest to keep the Christians divided. They treated the heretics as separate communities and encouraged them to maintain their own hierarchies. The Orthodox Patriarchates of Alexandria, Antioch, and Jerusalem continued to exist, but with reduced congregations and under the lay control of infidel masters. Though the Emperor at Constantinople still considered himself to be responsible for the welfare of the Orthodox all over the world, and though the Orthodox considered him as their true sovereign, even though they lived under the Caliph's rule, yet in practice it was impossible for the Eastern Patriarchs to keep in regular communication with the Imperial Court. For the next three centuries scarcely one of them was able to send on his election a Systatic Letter to his brother of Constantinople.[1] It was still more difficult to maintain any connexion with Rome, except through the rare pilgrims from the West. The practical elimination of his ancient rivals left the Patriarch of Constantinople the unquestioned head of Eastern Christendom. The rivalry between the Patriarchs became simply the rivalry between Rome and Constantinople; and, while Rome as a city was decaying as a result of the wars and invasions that Italy had undergone, Constantinople, the Imperial capital, was now by far the wealthiest, the most populous, and the most highly civilized city in Christendom. It was inevitable that its hierarchs should begin to resent or to ignore the ancient claims of the Bishop of

[1] According to Eutychius of Alexandria (*M.P.G.*, vol. cxi, col. 1156) no Patriarch of Constantinople was commemorated in the diptychs of Jerusalem or Alexandria between the Arab conquest and 937. Yahya of Antioch (*Patrologia Orientalis*, vol. xviii, pp. 706–8) confirms this and adds that the Pope was not commemorated between 683 and 999, for lack of information. These statements are probably exaggerated, as Constantinople and the Eastern Patriarchates were certainly in communication with each other during the Iconoclastic controversy and in the time of Photius, and Rome was in touch with Jerusalem fitfully from Charlemagne's day onwards. But there were probably large gaps in the diptychs, owing to the non-arrival of enthronization letters.

Rome. But at the same time the very chaos of the West added to the prestige of the Pope as the head of the one permanent institution there. The career of Gregory the Great showed how far-reaching the influence of the Papacy could be in the hands of an able and vigorous administrator.

Moreover, Rome still had a part to play in the politics of Constantinople. When the Isaurian Emperors imposed their Iconoclastic doctrine on the Empire and obliged the Patriarchs to co-operate with them, the opposition appealed to leading theologians outside the Empire, such as Saint John of Damascus, and hoped for particular support from the Pope, whose authority they emphasized in order to embarrass the Emperor and the Patriarch. The Pope duly denounced Iconoclasm as an error, but took small initiative in opposing it. His resentment against the Emperor was, rather, aroused when Leo III transferred the provinces of Sicily and Illyricum from the Patriarchate of Rome to that of Constantinople. The transference was not made because of the Roman refusal to obey the Iconoclastic decrees; indeed, the Emperor made no attempt to force Iconoclasm on either province. It was part of the general Isaurian scheme for tidying the administration of the Empire. The Emperor no longer had effective control over Rome and Italy, except precariously over Ravenna. But Sicily and Illyricum were Imperial provinces. It was only logical to make the territory of the Constantinopolitan Patriarchate coextensive with that governed by the lay authority of the Empire. Rome protested, but did not break off relations with Constantinople. The Pope's political position in Italy, threatened as it was by the Lombards, was not sure enough for him to dispense with Imperial aid. Twenty years later in 753, at the very moment when Constantine V was known to be holding his great Iconoclastic Council, Pope Stephen II sent an urgent appeal to Constantinople to beg for military assistance; and it was only because of Constantine's refusal to help him that he turned instead to the Franks and inaugurated the policy that was to lead to Charles the Great's Imperial coronation.[1] The Papacy was soon to find that Carolingian theology was almost as Iconoclastic as Isaurian, and the Carolingians were far more eager to interfere in religious matters at Rome than the Byzantines. Nor were relations broken off when Pope Leo III crowned Charles as Emperor. His action was resented at Constantinople, but it was also resented in many circles at Rome.[2]

The first Iconoclastic period ended with the Seventh Oecumenical Council in 787. The Empress Irene, who summoned it, invited delegates from Rome; and, as at Chalcedon, the Pope's statement of faith was made the basis for discussion and was accepted with minor additions. There was a general reconciliation; but the Empress did not offer to transfer Sicily and Illyricum back to Rome.[3] Iconoclasm was reintroduced in 815 by the Emperor Leo the Armenian; and the opposition, led by the monks of the monastery of Studium, maintained, in their desire to free the Church from Imperial control, that in an emergency the Pope, over whom the Emperor now had no control, should act as supreme authority. Studite theology triumphed, but not Studite ecclesiastical theory, which seemed to most Byzantines to be exaggerated and unwise. The Empress Theodora restored image-worship in 843 without any reference to Rome.[4]

[1] See Ostrogorsky, *Geschichte des Byzantinischen Staates*, pp. 125–33.

[2] See Ostrogorsky, op. cit., pp. 148–51, 160–2.

[3] Hefele–Leclercq, op. cit. iii. 2, pp. 741–98.

[4] Hefele–Leclercq, op. cit. iv. 1, pp. 110–15; Bury, *Eastern Roman Empire*, pp. 147–53. Theodore the Studite's views were not always consistent. His letters to Rome suggest that he regarded the Pope as supreme arbiter on doctrine and discipline, but to the Emperor he says that an appeal must be made to Rome because Constantinople has been unable to settle the matter by itself (letter ii. 86, *M.P.G.*, vol. xcix, col. 1332), while in a private letter (i. 28, ibid., col. 1001) he remarks: 'What is it to us what Rome does?' His views may have been affected by the Pope's refusal to come down strongly enough on his own side. See his letter, i. 34, ibid., col. 1021.

Soon afterwards there followed the disputes connected with the career of the Patriarch Photius. Till recent times Western historians regarded Photius as the arch-enemy of Rome, while to the East he was the champion of ecclesiastical nationalism. Modern research has proved that such simple views are wrong. While it is difficult fully to endorse the present tendency among historians to regard Photius as a high-minded man whose desire to be deferential to the Holy See was only thwarted by the tactlessness of Pope Nicholas I, yet the disputes ended with Rome and Constantinople, temporarily, at least, on better terms with each other than at their outset. But in the course of them the Patriarch had raised an issue which was to cause infinite bitterness for the future.[1]

In 847 the Empress Theodora appointed as Patriarch Ignatius, son of the Emperor Michael Rhangabe, who had been castrated at the time of his father's fall and had been brought up as a Studite monk. He was a stern narrow-minded moralist, who affected to despise intellectual achievements. Shortly after his appointment he had occasion to suspend the Archbishop of Syracuse, Gregory Asbestas, for certain irregularities. Gregory at once appealed to Rome, and incidentally cast doubts on the canonicity of Ignatius's election. As Syracuse was in a province arbitrarily transferred from Rome to Constaninople a century before, the appeal was calculated to cause trouble. The Pope demanded to be shown the acts of the synod that condemned Gregory. Ignatius, in spite of his Studite upbringing, refused to admit Rome's right to interfere. The dispute dragged on; and meanwhile the Empress was re-

[1] The following account is necessarily based on Dvornik's *Photian Schism*. Dr. Dvornik is inclined, I think, to minimize the differences between Photius and the Papacy, especially over the *Filioque* and its connexion with German influences at Rome. But his main thesis, that there was no second 'Photian Schism', is undoubtedly valid. See also the various articles by Grumel in *Échos d'Orient*, vols. xxix, xxxiii, xxxiv, xxxvii, xxxix (1930, 1934, 1935, 1938, 1940).

moved from the regency by her son, Michael III, who disliked Ignatius as his mother's friend and as a fearless critic of his own private life. In 858 he deposed Ignatius and appointed in his place a leading lay scholar, Photius. Photius, who was hastily rushed through the necessary stages of ordination, was determined to act with traditional correctitude. The practice of sending Systatic Letters on election had lapsed. Communications with the Eastern sees had long been uncertain, while the interchange of professions of faith between Rome and Constantinople seems to have been abandoned during the Iconoclastic controversy. Photius managed to dispatch letters to his Eastern colleagues and to Rome. He undoubtedly hoped thereby to win sympathy from the other Churches of Christendom and so weaken the many friends of Ignatius in the Byzantine Church, and he was probably also anxious to guard against a revival of Iconoclasm. If he had calculated that the Pope's quarrel with Ignatius would automatically bring him papal support, he was to be disillusioned. Pope Nicholas I had been shocked by rumours of the sudden elevation of a layman to the Patriarchate, and he considered that the whole controversy between the two Patriarchs was a God-given opportunity for him to assert the authority of Rome over Constantinople. He refused to accept Photius's Systatic Letter, but, three years later, in 861, he sent legates to Constantinople to say that he would overlook any irregularities on condition that Illyricum and Sicily were restored to the Roman See. The demand was ingeniously timed. The two great powers of central and eastern Europe were Moravia and Bulgaria, both of them pagan lands whose rulers were toying with the idea of conversion to Christianity. Half of Bulgaria lay within the old Illyrian province, as did much of Moravia. The retrocession of the province would therefore not only upset the administration of large parts of the Empire but it would prevent the expansion of Byzantine influence through missionary activity.

Neither Photius nor the Emperor could contemplate granting such a request. Instead, to show his goodwill, Photius suggested to the legates that in the name of the Pope they should arbitrate between him and Ignatius, and he would abide by their decision. The legates, who ought to have sent to Rome for instructions, agreed at once, thinking that they had scored a victory for their master. As Photius had foreseen, they decided in his favour, and confirmed the deposition of Ignatius. While Ignatius protested that he could not be bound by an arbitration to which he had not consented, Photius made it clear that his own submission had been voluntary and that it was not an acknowledgement of Rome's right to arbitrate. Pope Nicholas understood this. When his legates returned and told him of their success he angrily repudiated their action and refused to recognize Photius as Patriarch. There was schism between the two hierarchs.

It was during this schism that Moravia and Bulgaria were converted to Christianity by missionaries sent from Constantinople. In Moravia the missionaries decided that for geographical and political reasons the Churches that they founded must depend upon Rome. Their work was at first enthusiastically encouraged by the Popes but was repudiated later owing to the influence of the German Church. In Bulgaria King Boris first accepted the ecclesiastical domination of Byzantium, then turned to see if he could obtain better terms from Rome. Pope Nicholas sent one of his most trusted bishops, Formosus of Porto, to reorganize the new Bulgarian Church. This was an alarming set-back to Byzantine diplomacy; and soon reports reached Constantinople that Formosus was fiercely attacking the rules about the marriage of clergy and the Lenten Fast which the Byzantines had introduced into Bulgaria, and that he was insisting on the addition of the word *Filioque* to the Nicene Creed.

Photius was not a narrow-minded man. He held that

every Church had the right to follow its own usages, so long as it showed respect to those of other Churches. At the same time he relished a good discussion on theology. In his secular days, when he heard that Ignatius disdained the use of logic, he had invented a little heresy just to see how the worthy Patriarch would deal with it without the use of such aids.[1] He now discovered that Formosus was not only showing an un-Christian intolerance in Bulgaria, but was advocating an addition to the Creed which was, he considered, theologically erroneous and historically and ecclesiastically unwarranted, and which represented the victory of German influences at Rome. He eagerly took up his pen to inform the Eastern Patriarchs of these enormities.[2]

In September 867 the Emperor Michael III was murdered by his former protégé, Basil the Macedonian, who seized the throne. He at once deposed Photius and restored Ignatius to the Patriarchate. About the same time Pope Nicholas died and was succeeded by Hadrian II, who personally disliked Formosus and the German party that he represented. When Ignatius sought a reconciliation with Rome, Hadrian gladly responded and sent delegates to attend a council to be held in Constantinople in 869. But the council did not go well. The Roman legates hoped to induce the assembled bishops to sign a *libellus* declaring that the Faith was kept inviolate by the Holy See; but the Imperial authorities intervened and forbade its signature. Instead, the council voted against the legates that the concurrence of all five Patriarchs was needed on matters of theology. When the question of the Bulgarian Church arose the legates were again outvoted. The council ordained that it

[1] Anecdote reported by St. Constantine-Cyril to Anastasius the Librarian, in Mansi, *Sacrorum Conciliorum Collectio*, vol. xvi, col. 6. Dvornik, op. cit., pp. 32–33, regards the story as having been invented by Photius's enemies.

[2] Photius, letter I. 13; *M.P.G.*, vol. cii, coll. 722–41. Photius's attitude was certainly to be explained by the fear felt by the Byzantines of German influences at Rome and in the Balkans.

was for the Emperor to decide to which Patriarchate Bulgaria belonged; and he naturally assigned it to Constantinople, knowing that King Boris had by now come to the conclusion that Rome was too strict a mistress for his tastes. Photius was indeed labelled as a usurper; but Ignatius proved himself even more intractable. So, though Pope and Patriarch were once more officially in communion, relations between them were very cold. The Pope was about to excommunicate Ignatius when news arrived of his death in 877.

To succeed Ignatius the Emperor Basil surprisingly reappointed Photius, whose ability he had come to appreciate. Photius was eager to make peace with Rome; and he found the Pope, John VIII, who had been elected in 872, equally desirous of a settlement. A new council was held at Constantinople in 879. The acts of the council of 869 were annulled. Photius was recognized as legitimate Patriarch. The perfect orthodoxy of Rome was stated, though, had the legates understood Greek better, they might have objected to a clause anathematizing all who added to the Nicene Creed, that is to say, large sections of the Church of Rome. The Emperor was in mourning and did not attend the meetings, but Photius brought a gracious message from him assigning the Bulgarian Church to Rome. The council ended with mutual expressions of goodwill and a tactful silence about disputed usages; and the language used by Photius towards the Pope was as deferential as Roman tradition required. The only drawback was the refusal of King Boris of Bulgaria to submit his Church to Rome. As Photius and the Emperor were well aware, he intended to remain within the jurisdiction of Constantinople; but they could not be blamed for his decision.

The Photian episode thus ended with a complete reconciliation between the Papacy and the Patriarchate. It is true that friends of Ignatius hurried to Rome and, in alliance with the German party there, did such propaganda that in time it came to be believed that there was another schism and Photius had been excommunicated; and it is true that Formosus when he eventually became Pope attempted to upset the settlement; but his Papacy was short and disastrous. For many decades to come there was peace within the Universal Church. When, early in the tenth century, a schism developed within the Byzantine Church over the fourth marriage of the Emperor Leo VI, the tact of the victorious Patriarch and the restraint of the Pope were alike admirable.[1] Meanwhile the Carolingian Empire was dying, and German influence at Rome was dormant. The Byzantines, though they had just lost Sicily to the Moslems, had in the last years of the ninth century revived their hold over southern Italy. From 904 to 962 Rome itself was ruled by a native patrician family, the House of Theophylact, whose policy was friendship with Byzantium and whose puppet-Popes were not permitted to endanger the alliance. In this atmosphere of goodwill the Emperor gladly allowed the Roman See in 924 to take over the province of Dalmatia, with its Latin-speaking Churches, though it was part of Illyricum.

The prospects for lasting peace seemed favourable. But in fact none of the old controversies and problems had been solved; and there was now the newer issue that Photius had remarked. Increasing numbers of Western Christians were adopting the addition to the Creed which he had denounced. It only needed a political revolution in Italy for the whole quarrel to flare up again in a fiercer and more fateful form than before. The spark was lit by the restoration of the Western Empire.

[1] See Ostrogorsky, op. cit., pp. 208–9, 219; Dvornik, op. cit., pp. 275 ff.

II

MICHAEL CERULARIUS

In 962 Otto the Saxon, King of Germany, led an army through Italy to Rome and forced the reluctant Pope, John XII, to crown him Emperor. For the next forty years Rome was the scene of a struggle between the Germans and the native nobility, led by the House of Crescentius, kin to the House of Theophylact, which enjoyed the sympathy of the Byzantines.[1] But Byzantium was engrossed by civil wars and wars of reconquest in the East and the Balkans. It took no active interest in Italy, except when the Germans tried to invade its provinces in the south. In Rome the Germans eventually established their authority; and their victory meant first that ideas originating north of the Alps for reforming the Church began to be tried out at Rome, and secondly that German theology triumphed there.

There were now two great movements for reform in the Western Church. One was centred in Lorraine; and its leaders' aim was to concentrate on the episcopacy, abolishing simony and the appointment of unsuitable bishops, to insist on the celibacy of the clergy, and in general to tighten ecclesiastical discipline. The Lorrainers were glad to use the help of the lay authorities, and they soon won the support of the German Emperors, who saw that an efficient hierarchy would be of great value to their administration. The Emperors intended to control Rome and so were ready to enhance the disciplinary powers of the Roman See. The second centre of reform was the Abbey of Cluny, whose aim was to restore a high standard to monastic life. The Cluniacs continually found their efforts thwarted by local

[1] See Gay, *L'Italie méridionale et l'Empire byzantin*, pp. 218–28.

interests. They therefore placed their Order under the direct control of the Bishop of Rome. It was in consequence essential to them that the authority of the Pope should override all other ecclesiastical authorities. Both schools of reform were interested in reasserting the full historic claims of the Roman See.[1]

The triumph of German theology meant the addition of the word *Filioque* to the Creed. The Nicene Fathers had declared that the Holy Ghost proceeds from the Father; but for many centuries there had been congregations in the West who believed it to be more correct to say that the Procession was from the Father and the Son. The addition seems first to have appeared in Spain, in the course of the disputes between the Spanish Catholics and the Arian Visigoths. It was inserted in the so-called Athanasian Creed, promulgated by the Spaniards in the seventh century; and when they adopted the Nicene Creed soon afterwards they retained the word.[2] From Spain it found its way to the Carolingian Court and found an eager advocate in Charles the Great, who tried to impose it on the Papacy.[3] In 808 the Patriarch of Jerusalem wrote to Pope Leo III to complain that Frankish Benedictine monks on the Mount of Olives were adding the *Filioque* to the Creed. As Charles was paying for these monks, Leo passed the complaint on to him, commenting that while he thought the theological

[1] The best modern account of the reform of the Western Church is given by A. Dumas in Fliche et Martin, *Histoire de l'Église*, vol. vii, book iii, and by A. Fliche, ibid., vol. viii, chapters i–iii. The idea of papal universal rule is already contained in the propaganda issued by the followers of Pope Symmachus in the early sixth century and in the Donation of Constantine in the eighth century, and is clearly expressed by Walafrid Strabo in the ninth century (*M.P.L.*, vol. cxiv, coll. 963–6).

[2] See Palmieri, article 'Filioque', in Vacant et Mangenot, *Dictionnaire de Théologie Catholique*, vol. v. 2, coll. 2309 ff. It is doubtful whether the clause was inserted in the Acts of the First Council of Toledo (400), but it certainly appeared in those of the Fourth Council there (633).

[3] The Council of Frankfort (794) adopted the formula, and criticized the Patriarch Tarasius of Constantinople for using the formula *per Filium*. Hefele–Leclercq, *Histoire des Conciles*, iii. 2, pp. 1061–91.

implications of the addition to be unobjectionable and indeed to suit the Western tradition, it was a mistake to depart from the version of the Creed that had been universally accepted by Christendom.[1] When he himself inscribed the Creed on silver plaques round the interior of Saint Peter's he omitted the word.[2] In the course of the ninth century it was generally adopted by the Church in Germany and Lorraine, and by many Churches in France, though Paris retained the original form for another two centuries.[3] German ecclesiastics brought it to Rome, where Formosus, amongst others, accepted it. He in his turn introduced it into Bulgaria, and so to the notice of Photius, who at once protested against it. John VIII took the same line as Leo III. He considered that it was impolitic to change the Creed, but he saw no theological objection to the word itself.[4] The revival of German influence at Rome in the late tenth century meant the reappearance there of the *Filioque*, whose insertion came gradually to be accepted as part of the official doctrine. We know that it occurred in the Creed that was formally sung at the coronation of the Emperor Henry II in 1014.[5]

The dispute over the *Filioque* was to produce a vast and passionate crop of polemical preaching and writing, most of which seems to us today unreal and off the point. The

[1] Pope Leo's correspondence on the subject is given in *M.P.L.*, vol. cxxix, coll. 1257–60, and his reply to the Frankish ambassadors in Smaragdus, *M.P.L.*, vol. cii, coll. 971–6. See also *M.P.G.*, vol. xciv, coll. 205–8, *Dissertationes Damascenicae*, i, reporting the episode, and Hefele–Leclercq, op. cit. iii. 2, pp. 1127–31.

[2] *Liber Pontificalis*, ed. Duchesne, ii, p. 26.

[3] For Paris, see Alexander of Hales, *Summa Theologica* (Cologne edition), i, p. 218.

[4] See above, notes 1 and 2, also Dvornik, *The Photian Schism*, pp. 122, 196, 444.

[5] Pope Christopher (903–4) is said by the Chartophylax Nicetas to have added the *Filioque* to the Creed in his Systatic Letter to Nicholas Mysticus, who therefore refused to recognize him. See below, p. 33, n. 1. For its appearance in 1014 see Berno of Reichenau, *M.P.L.*, vol. cxlii, coll. 1060–1. Berno was present at the ceremony.

protagonists, indeed, seldom answered each others' arguments fairly. This was inevitable; for the fundamental difference between Eastern and Western theology lay deeper. The Western argument was that the word *Filioque* merely gave precision to a doctrine that was inherent in the Creed. This was undoubtedly correct and in accordance with Western theological tradition, which had always envisaged as its chief enemy the Arianism of the Goths and therefore tended to maintain that the Trinity was a single interchangeable hypostasis. But Eastern theological tradition had developed out of the fierce Christological controversies of the fifth and sixth centuries. To guard against the heresies of Nestorianism on one side and Eutychianism on the other, it held the Trinity to be composed of three Persons with separate properties joined in one hypostatic union, and interpreted the Nicene Creed in that light; and it emphasized the omnipresent and pervasive nature of the Holy Spirit. The introduction of the *Filioque* upset the delicate balance of properties within the Trinity. It was permissible to say that the Holy Ghost descended through the Son, but no more. Photius was therefore justified according to his lights when he declared that the new addition seemed to him to savour either of Manichaeanism in that it divided the Creator into two principles or alternatively of Neoplatonism in that it introduced a ladder of divine Beings. But to his opponents his arguments genuinely seemed irrelevant. Unfortunately few of the disputants ever realized that the real issue was over the nature of the Trinity.[1] Had there been greater mutual comprehension it

[1] St. Augustine already realized that there was a difference between the Eastern and Western conception of the Trinity (*De Trinitate*, vii. 4, *M.P.L.*, vol. xlii, coll. 939–42). St. Anselm says, a little over-simply, that the Latins talk of one Substance and three Persons, and the Greeks of one Person and three Substances (letter to Rainald, *M.P.L.*, vol. clviii, col. 1144; *De Fide Trinitatis*, ibid., col. 284). It is perhaps truer to say that the Western view is that the unity of God is absolute and the Persons of the Trinity are relative within it, while the Eastern view is that the three Persons have each a distinctive property but are joined in a

might have been possible to cover over the theological difference. The Westerners from the very nature of their argument could not object if certain Churches chose to omit the disputed word; while the Eastern Churches believed in the propriety of showing Economy or charity towards those Christians whose doctrines diverged from their own but were not definitely pronounced heretical. But behind the theological issue lay another about which the East felt even more strongly. The Creed had been issued by an Oecumenical Council, which was in Eastern eyes the one inspired doctrinal authority. To add to the Creed was to question the authority and inspiration of the Fathers of the Church. Only another Oecumenical Council had the right, not indeed to alter, but to amplify and explain the decisions reached at an earlier council. If the Western Churches tampered unilaterally with the Creed of the councils they must thereby automatically lapse into heresy; nor would any pronouncement by the Pope in their favour serve to condone them. The East saw in the dispute a direct attack on its whole theory of Church government and doctrine.

If we choose to date the final schism between Rome and Constantinople from the last mention of a Roman Pope in the diptychs of Constantinople, then the schism occurred in 1009. The last Pope whose name was recorded at Constantinople was John XVIII, who died that year. His successor, Sergius IV, sent a Systatic Letter to Constantinople; but, probably because his declaration of faith included the *Filioque* in the Creed, the Patriarch, whose name was also Sergius, rejected it and refused to include his name in

hypostatic union. Every, *The Byzantine Patriarchate*, p. 87 (a sympathetic account of the basic difference), goes a little far in saying that Greek theologians taught that each of the Persons has his own hypostasis. They made a point of stressing the one hypostasis—τὴν μίαν τῆς ἁγίας τρίαδος ὑπόστασιν—as Peter of Antioch inserts in his declaration of faith to his fellow Patriarchs. (See his letters in Michel, *Humbert und Kerullarios*, ii, pp. 432–54.) A fair-minded account of the actual doctrines about the *Filioque* at the end of the eleventh century is given in Leib, *Rome, Kiev et Byzance*, pp. 331–44.

the diptychs.[1] As it happened, no Pope was ever mentioned there again. We must not exaggerate the significance of this. The lists on the diptychs were necessarily incomplete. For many generations Constantinople had received no Systatic Letters from the Eastern Patriarchates, despite the full communion between them. It was not till the end of the ninth century that the improvement of international communications allowed the hierarchs to keep in regular touch with each other. The names of the Popes were commemorated at Constantinople from the time of the Photian dispute till the close of the tenth century; but there had been gaps before the time of Pope Sergius IV. In 996 the Western Emperor Otto III gave Rome its first German Pope in the person of his young cousin Bruno, Gregory V, who was not commemorated at Constantinople, presumably because as a German he made use of the *Filioque*. Gregory, who was a foolish boy, was soon ejected by the Romans, who elected in his stead Otto's former tutor, the Greek John Philagathus, John XVI, who sent a Systatic Letter to Constantinople and was commemorated there. Otto returned in wrath and reinstated Gregory, after capturing and mutilating John. When Gregory died, Otto gave

[1] Two alternative texts attributed to the Chartophylax Nicetas of Nicaea tell, one of Pope Christopher's insertion of the *Filioque* and its continued adoption by Popes Sergius III and IV, and the other, more vaguely, of a 'schism between the two Sergii', of which the author says 'I do not know the cause'. The texts are given in Michel, *Humbert und Kerullarius*, ii, pp. 20–40, and the second is printed also in *M.P.G.*, vol. cxx, coll. 713 ff. The whole treatise, which deals with recent schisms between Rome and Constantinople, is critical of the Greeks. It is difficult to believe that it was written by Nicetas of Nicaea, whose other works show him to have been distinctly anti-Latin (see Krumbacher, *Geschichte des Byzantinischen Litteratur*, pp. 81–82). I would suggest that it was an early work of Nicetas of Maronea, later Archbishop of Thessalonica and a supporter of the Emperor Manuel Comnenus's conciliatory policy, written when he was Chartophylax of Constantinople, and that an error had some time been made in the manuscript heading. Jugie, *Le Schisme Byzantin*, pp. 166–7, does not believe that the 'schism between the Sergii' concerned the *Filioque*, but the first alternative text of Nicetas seems to suggest it. See Michel, op. cit. i, pp. 20–23.

Rome its first French Pope, Gerbert of Aurillac, Sylvester II, who was not named in the Constantinopolitan diptychs. John XVIII, like John XVI, was the nominee of the Crescentian party.[1] It seems therefore that the Popes appointed by German influence were not commemorated at Constantinople, presumably because of their German theology; but it may be that they never troubled to send a Systatic Letter there. Sergius IV definitely sent a letter which was rejected. A century later it was remembered at Constantinople that there had been a 'schism of the two Sergii', but scarcely anyone knew then what the reason for it had been, and it was believed to have been of short duration.[2] We must remember the Eastern point of view, which differentiated between the bishopric and the person of the bishop. Pope Sergius had branded himself a heretic, but in default of further evidence it might be assumed that his heresy ended with his death. His successors, who prudently failed to send a declaration of faith to Constantinople, might be regarded as Orthodox, even though they had not taken the formal step which would enable their brothers of Constantinople to commemorate them.

In spite of the difference over the Creed, which was the first symptom of dangers likely to arise in the future, there was in the early eleventh century no feeling that the unity of Christendom had been broken nor any desire for a break. On the contrary, the peoples of Christendom were in closer touch with each other than they had been since the first barbarian invasions. This renewed intimacy was to cause trouble when it came to be discovered that during the intervening centuries the different peoples had developed divergent customs and theories; but, for the moment, ill feeling was confined to a few hierarchs. The pilgrim traffic was reaching its zenith. With the Byzantine recapture of Crete in 961 the eastern Mediterranean became safe for Christian

[1] See Michel, op. cit. i, p. 16; also Gay, op. cit., pp. 387–98.

[2] See above, p. 33, n. 1.

ships. Antioch was recovered in 969, and soon Byzantium was in control of northern Syria. Southern Syria and Palestine passed to the rule of the Fatimid Caliphs of Egypt, who with the exception of the mad Caliph Hakim were tolerant and friendly and well aware of the financial advantages brought by Christian merchants and visitors. Italian merchant-colonies were established in Eastern lands. The formation of the Varangian Guard brought the Byzantine Emperor into permanent and intimate touch with Westerners. Every year increasing numbers of Western Christians set out to pay their respects at the shrines of the Holy Land; and many of them paused at Constantinople to admire the great collections of relics there. The Byzantine reconquest of the Balkans in the early eleventh century opened up a cheap land-route. A pilgrim coming through Hungary or Croatia had only two frontiers to cross between central Europe and Palestine. Antioch and Jerusalem now maintained a constant connexion with the West, and even Alexandria, which had become the feeblest and most isolated of the Orthodox Patriarchates, could renew her long-lost contacts.[1] In Italy itself Greek monks from Calabria, of whom the most eminent example was Saint Nilus, Abbot of Grottaferrata, and the most unfortunate was John Philagathus, served as a liaison between the Byzantine Church and Rome.[2]

Unfortunately for the Eastern Churches the restoration of communications coincided with the growth of the reform movement at Rome. The Cluniacs were particularly interested in the pilgrim traffic, which they largely helped to organize; and they were the strongest advocates of the universal claims of Rome. The Byzantines were conscious of the problem. In 1024 the Patriarch Eustathius of

[1] See above, p. 19, n. 1. For the pilgrim traffic, see Runciman, *History of the Crusades*, i, pp. 38 ff.

[2] The Life of St. Nilus of Calabria is published in *M.P.G.*, vol. cxx. For John Philagathus, see Gay, op. cit., pp. 391–5.

Constantinople, with the backing of the Emperor Basil II, wrote to Pope John XIX suggesting that the time had come to settle once and for all the relations of their two sees; and he proposed a formula that 'with the consent of the Roman bishop the Church of Constantinople shall be called and considered universal in her own sphere, as that of Rome is in the world'. The original Greek words have not survived; but it seems clear that the Patriarch intended that his Patriarchate should be admitted to be self-sufficient and autonomous, while the primacy of Rome was to be recognized and Rome was to remain the suitable court to which to apply for arbitration and information. It has been suggested that the Patriarch's motive was to heal the schism of the two Sergii; but more probably he was anxious to establish his authority over the Churches in the Byzantine provinces of southern Italy, where trouble was beginning to occur. As Byzantium was now at the height of its power and the Papacy had sunk to a low level, he doubtless thought his proposal generous; and John XIX apparently agreed to it. But at once there was an outcry amongst the Cluniacs; and the Abbot of Saint-Benignus at Dijon wrote angrily to reprove the Pope for his lack of vigour in governing the Universal Church and to remind him that, though the secular Empire might be divided up between many rulers, the domain of Saint Peter was indivisible. The heir of Saint Peter could not parcel out his power to bind and to loose. Pope John withdrew his agreement; and in consequence his name was never mentioned in the diptychs of Constantinople nor in the Synodicon published there in 1025.[1] It was probably the news of this unsuccessful *démarche* and the fury that it caused beyond the Alps that inspired a faraway German chronicler to write in the year 1028, the year after Pope John had crowned Conrad the Salic as Emperor, that

[1] The story of the Byzantine *démarche* is given by Radulf Glaber, *M.P.L.*, vol. cxlii, col. 671. The Synodicon of 1025 is published in Michel, op. cit. i, p. 25.

this was when, in his words, 'the Eastern Church withdrew itself from obedience to the Holy See'.[1]

These words are incorrect and misleading. It is true that the episode must have alarmed Constantinople about the nature of papal claims; but it had altered nothing in fact. The Pope and the Patriarch of Constantinople continued to omit each other's names in their diptychs; but the Patriarch of Antioch, though he was the subject of the Byzantine Emperor, seems to have continued to commemorate the Pope, ignoring the difference over the *Filioque*, and it is probable that the Patriarch of Jerusalem did likewise.[2] Latin churches, for the use of the Varangians and Latin pilgrims, remained open at Constantinople. Westerners freely worshipped at Byzantine shrines. There was a Latin, Amalfitan, monastery on Mount Athos.[3] Coolness only existed between the two supreme hierarchs. But the situation was inflammable; and soon political events were to add another and very dangerous spark.

The Byzantine Empire now officially controlled all Italy south of a line drawn from Terracina on the Tyrrhenian Sea to Termoli on the Adriatic. Within this area there were two Lombard principalities, Salerno and Capua-Benevento, whose rulers seldom showed much deference to their Imperial suzerain, and three self-governing merchant-cities, Gaeta, Naples, and Amalfi, of which only Amalfi was a consistently dutiful vassal, finding considerable commercial advantage in the vassalage. There were also two provinces under direct Byzantine rule—Calabria, where the population was entirely Greek, and Apulia or 'Langobardia', where the cities, such as the metropolis Bari, were mainly Greek, but the countryside largely Lombard and Latin. The Patriarch of Constantinople never attempted assert his authority over the Latin vassal-states, though to

[1] *Chronica S. Petri Erphordensis moderna, M.G.H.Ss.*, vol. xxx, p. 407; *Chronica minor auctore minorita Erphordensis*, ibid., vol. xxiv, p. 189.

[2] See below, pp. 65, 69. [3] Leib, op. cit., pp. 82–83, 100–1.

there were Greek churches at Naples and Amalfi. But Apulia was a different matter. There, Greek and Latin churches existed side by side; and while the Greeks looked to Constantinople for guidance, the Latins could not help looking to Rome, just across the frontier.[1]

In 1020 an Apulian called Melo raised a revolt in southern Italy against Byzantium, and in the course of it he hired the services of some Norman knights who had come to pay a pilgrimage to their favourite shrine of Saint Michael on Monte Gargano. Melo's revolt was suppressed, in spite of help given him by the Western Emperor. But the Normans stayed and summoned their friends and relations from northern France. From 1040 onward the remarkable family of Hauteville set about the systematic conquest of the whole of southern Italy, Byzantine and Lombard alike; and not only Constantinople but also Rome had to consider what might happen should the Hautevilles be successful. The Western Emperor at this time was Henry III, a man who combined great energy and ability with deep piety and an earnest desire to complete the reform of the Church. When he arrived in Italy in 1046 he found no less than three rival Popes fighting for the control of Rome. He deposed them all and gave the papal throne to a respectable German, Clement II. Neither Clement nor his successor Damasus lived long; and in 1048 Henry bestowed the Papacy on a distinguished Lorrainer, Bruno, Bishop of Toul, who became Pope Leo IX. Henry soon was too fully occupied in Germany to return to Italy; and Pope Leo was left to handle Italian affairs as he thought best.

Meanwhile the Normans were steadily increasing their power in the south. The Papacy had not much regretted their first victories over the Byzantines; for though they were freebooters, they were members of the Latin Church. But when they began to overrun the Lombard principalities and to approach the frontiers of Rome, Leo, who knew that

[1] Gay, op. cit., pp. 414–29.

no help would reach him from Germany, decided that it would be wise to ally himself with the Byzantine Emperor to suppress them. About the same time the Emperor appointed a distinguished Lombard, Argyrus, son of the former rebel, Melo, to the command of the Imperial troops in Italy. He as a Latin was naturally sympathetic to the idea of an alliance with Rome, and considered that it would be politically wise.[1]

There was, however, one difficulty to be overcome. The Normans were after all Latins, and the districts that they occupied were thereby brought under Latin ecclesiastical domination. The Pope had no intention of letting them revert to Byzantine rule; and he wished also to be sure that all the Churches there should conform to Roman usages. Hitherto the great Churches of Christendom had not been greatly troubled over divergencies of usage. The Byzantines, devoted though they were to their own liturgy, recognized that other Churches might follow other customs. There had been in the past many varied practices within the great Patriarchate of the West. But the reformed Papacy was anxious, in the interest of discipline and order, to introduce uniformity of usage; and there were signs of a similar trend at Constantinople. Any attack on Greek usages in the West might therefore provoke a counter-attack in the East.[2]

The Byzantine Emperor, Constantine IX, had confidence in Argyrus and favoured an alliance with Rome. But the Patriarch of Constantinople thought otherwise. Michael Cerularius, who now enters on the scene, had been appointed to the patriarchal throne in 1043. He was a retired civil servant, who had taken orders late in life. He was an able and vigorous administrator, but he had the rigid mind of a civil servant; nor was he well versed in theology or Church history. He had none of the subtlety and wit nor

[1] Gay, op. cit., pp. 433 ff.; Chalandon, *La Domination normande en Sicile*, i, pp. 1–188.

[2] See below, p. 41.

the wide culture that characterized Photius, though, like Photius, he took a deep interest in occultism. He was arrogant and very ambitious, both for himself and for his see. To the historian he is not an attractive figure; but in fact he enjoyed immense popularity at Constantinople, where his influence was far greater than that of the amiable but somewhat eccentric Emperor.[1]

To understand the part that Cerularius now played we must remember, first, that he had some knowledge of recent events at Rome and had derived from them a not unnatural contempt for the Papacy. Secondly he personally disliked and distrusted Argyrus, whose influence over the Emperor he resented, and whose parentage and past history roused his suspicion. Thirdly, with his tidy bureaucratic mind he was as eager as any reforming Pope to introduce a uniformity of usages within his Patriarchate. In this he may have been inspired by Western examples; but he was not primarily concerned with the Latin world. The Empire had recently annexed the last independent Armenian principalities; and there was a general wish at Constantinople to integrate the Armenian Church into the official Church of the Empire. The Armenians were mildly

[1] For the career and character of Michael Cerularius, see Amann, article 'Michel Cerulaire' in Vacant et Mangenot, *Dictionnaire de Théologie Catholique*, vol. x. 2, coll. 1677 ff., and Jugie, *Le Schisme byzantin*, pp. 187 ff. Both are severely critical of him. Gay, op. cit., esp. pp. 498–9, showed that he was not as insincere as had been claimed. There is no reliable contemporary account of him. Psellus delivered a denunciatory address against him before the Synod of 1059 and a laudatory funeral oration for him a few months later, neither of them completely convincing. (The former is ed. Bréhier in *Revue des Études grecques*, vol. xvi (1903), pp. 375–416, and vol. xvii (1904), pp. 35–76, the latter in Sathas, *Μεσαιωνικὴ Βιβλιοθήκη*, vol. iv, pp. 303–87.) The impression given by his recorded actions is of an arrogant and not very likeable man, but there is no doubt that he was immensely popular with the people of Constantinople. But a rather more sympathetic picture is given by the Nestorian Ibn Butlan, who wrote for Cerularius a treatise against the Azymites. See Graf, 'Die Eucharistielehre des Nestorianers al-Muhtar ibn Butlan,' in *Orient Christianus*, vol. xxxv (1938), pp. 44–70.

heretical. They had rejected the findings of the Council of Chalcedon, though their theology was Monothelete rather than Monophysite. Many of their usages differed entirely from those of the Greeks. Apart from their occasional liking for animal sacrifices, they began Lent at Septuagesima; they approved of fasting on Saturdays; and, most important of all, they used unleavened bread for the Sacrament. Such practices were considered by Greek theologians to be distinctly Judaistic; but unfortunately almost identical practices were followed by the Latins. It was pointless to forbid them to the Armenians if they could be seen in regular use in the Latin churches at Constantinople.[1] Cerularius was therefore eager for an excuse to force conformity on the Latin churches. When he discovered that the Normans, with the approval of Rome, were forbidding Greek usages in the areas that they now controlled, and that reforming synods throughout Italy were denouncing the various churches that for some reason or other still kept to Greek customs, he at once ordered the Latin churches at Constantinople to adopt Greek usages; and on their refusal he closed them, about the end of the year 1052.[2] He then induced Leo, Archbishop of Ochrida and head of the Bulgarian Church, to write a letter to John, Bishop of the Greek city of Trani in Apulia and *syncellus*, that is to say, patriarchal agent, in Italy, which he was to pass on to 'the most reverend Pope' and 'all the bishops of the Franks'. The letter consisted in the main of a fierce attack on the use of

[1] Every, op. cit., p. 166, suggesting that Cerularius's preoccupation with the azymes was due to his desire to force conformity on the Armenian churches. We may note that the Armenian Catholicus Peter was summoned to Constantinople by the Emperor in 1049. He was well received by the Emperor and the Patriarch; but general relations between the Byzantines and the Armenians soon worsened. (Michael of Edessa, i. 74, trans. Dulaurier, pp. 85–87.)

[2] Leo IX, letters 19 and 29, *M.P.L.*, vol. cxliii, coll. 758, 764; Humbert of Silva Candida, *Brevis et succincta Commemoratio*, ibid., col. 1002. Humbert accuses the Greek authorities of having provoked a riot when closing the churches and of having trampled the Host underfoot.

azymes, or unleavened bread, for the Sacrament, with appendixes denouncing the habit of fasting on Saturdays, of eating strangled meat, and of not singing alleluia in the days following on Septuagesima.[1]

This aggressive document arrived in Italy at an unfortunate moment. Argyrus and the Pope had arranged their alliance; but before their armies could meet Argyrus was defeated by the Normans in February 1053, and in June the papal army, with Leo at its head, was routed at Civitate, and the Pope was taken off to an honourable captivity at Benevento. The Normans had no wish to interrupt the running of the Church, so they gave permission to the chief Papal Secretary, Humbert of Mourmoutiers, Cardinal of Silva Candida, to join his master. Humbert did not go straight from Rome to Benevento, but travelled first into Apulia, probably to interview Argyrus there. As he passed through Trani, Bishop John handed him Leo of Ochrida's letter. Humbert knew a little Greek and hastily made a translation, which was probably not very accurate and exaggerated its already offensive tone. When he arrived at Benevento he laid the letter and the translation before the Pope. Leo was spending his enforced leisure in learning Greek; but it is doubtful if he knew enough to check Humbert's translation. In any case he was outraged. He had hoped for friendly co-operation from Byzantium; he had not expected a rude attack on the customs of his Church. He told Humbert to draft two replies in his name. One was addressed discourteously to the 'Bishops' Michael of Constantinople and Leo of Ochrida, and contained a disquisition on the supremacy of the Roman See, based on arguments taken from the Donation of Constantine. The second, whose addressee is not named, was a detailed defence of Latin usages.[2] The Pope may have thought

[1] Leo of Ochrida, *Epistola ad Ioannem Episcopum Tranensem, M.P.G.*, vol. cxx, coll. 836 ff. See Michel, op. cit. ii, pp. 282–91.

[2] Leo IX, *Epistola C ad Michaelem Constantinopolitanum, M.P.L.*, vol.

Humbert's language too stern; for the letters were not at once dispatched. Meanwhile a courier arrived from Constantinople with two letters very different in tone from the last. One, signed by the Emperor, cordially advocated a closer political alliance. The other, signed by Cerularius, prayed for closer unity between the Churches. No mention was made of disputed usages. Instead, the Patriarch promised to inscribe the Pope's name in the diptychs throughout the Empire, provided that his own name was inscribed at Rome. But, most regrettably, Cerularius addressed the Pope as 'Brother', not as 'Father', the title with which in the past Patriarchs had usually recognized the Pope's seniority; and he signed himself 'Oecumenical Patriarch'. And Leo's staff translated the Patriarch's word for Empire as the Universe.[1]

The Patriarch's remarkable change of tone is usually ascribed to the influence of the Emperor. This is hard to believe, for on no other occasion did Cerularius show the least deference to his sovereign's wishes. The peace-maker was almost certainly Bishop John of Trani, whom Argyrus had just sent to Constantinople to report on the Italian situation. The Patriarch could not doubt John of Trani's loyalty; and John persuaded him that the Pope was a distinguished and reasonable man, whose friendship was

cxliii, coll. 744–69; *Adversus Graecorum Calumnias*, ibid., coll. 931–74 (incorrectly entitled *Dialogus inter Romanum et Constantinopolitanum*). Michel, op. cit. i, pp. 43–76, shows that Humbert was the author.

[1] These letters are only known from the papal replies (see below, p. 44, n. 1) and from Cerularius's letter to Peter of Antioch (*M.P.G.*, vol. cxx, coll. 781–96). The Pope was deeply shocked (as is Père Jugie, op. cit., p. 188) because Cerularius offered, in return for having his name commemorated in the Roman Church, to see that the Pope's name was commemorated in the churches *in toto orbe terrarum*. But it is most unlikely that even Cerularius would have claimed to control the churches of the whole world. It seems clear that this is another case of mistranslation. Cerularius used the word *οἰκουμένη* in its Byzantine sense of 'the Empire' and the Romans translated it in its literal sense of 'the whole inhabited world'. It was a similar misunderstanding which caused the trouble over the title 'Oecumenical'.

necessary if anything was to be salvaged in Italy. Leo would have done wisely had he responded to the note of conciliation and ignored the Patriarch's haughty phrasing. But his health was failing, and he left the whole affair in the hands of Cardinal Humbert.[1]

If Cerularius is to be blamed for what followed, equal, if not greater, blame should be laid on Humbert. He was a man of some erudition and of genuine if narrow piety; but he was hot-tempered and truculent, and he disliked the Greeks. He decided that legates must be sent to Constantinople, and he drafted two more letters in the Pope's name for the legates to take with them. The first letter was to Cerularius. It repeated the arguments about the supremacy of the Holy See. It reproved the Patriarch for his use of the Oecumenical title. It cast doubts upon the canonicity of his election, it seems without any justification. It accused him of infringing the prerogatives of the Churches of Alexandria and Antioch, with perhaps some justification in the latter case. It remarked upon the impertinence of his criticism of Latin usages, especially of the use of unleavened bread; and it ended with the hope that the legates whom the Pope was sending to Constantinople would find him sincerely repentant. The second letter, addressed to the Emperor, complained of the Patriarch's behaviour and warned the Emperor that unless he were restrained reprisals would be taken. It asked the Emperor to give every assistance to the legates.[2]

The legates appointed by the Pope were Humbert himself, Frederick of Lorraine, Chancellor of the Roman See,

[1] Gay, op. cit., pp. 492–500, convincingly suggests the role played by John of Trani. Cerularius was in communication with him about the Pope's situation and his character (letter to Peter of Antioch, col. 788), and his volte-face and his subsequent reaction must have been due to his reliance on a report given by John.

[2] Jugie, op. cit., pp. 197–8; Gay, loc. cit., showing, as against Bréhier (*Le Schisme oriental*, pp. 97 ff.), that both batches of papal letters were brought by the legates in person to Constantinople. The text of the two later letters is given in *M.P.L.*, vol. cxliii, coll. 773–81.

and Peter, Archbishop of Amalfi, whose city was a vassal-state of the Empire and contained a large Greek population. They set out early in 1054 and paused in Apulia to interview Argyrus, who advised them to ignore the Patriarch and to treat only with the Emperor. It was foolish advice; for Cerularius was the more forceful and more popular figure. They arrived at Constantinople in April, bringing with them the Pope's two letters and a dossier containing his two previous unposted letters and a report from the Patriarchate of Jerusalem which showed that practices there differed from those of Constantinople.[1]

On their arrival the legates first called on the Patriarch. They were dissatisfied with the protocol of their reception; so they thrust the Pope's letter at the Patriarch and retired without giving him the customary salutations. When Cerularius opened the letter he was astounded. He had been assured by John of Trani that the Pope was a high-minded and sympathetic man who would respond to his friendly gesture; and here he was treated with discourtesy and abuse. He examined the seals of the letter and decided that someone had tampered with them. He at once concluded that the legates had shown the letter to Argyrus and that Argyrus had altered the text with their connivance. His first assumption was probably correct and would explain why the letter had been resealed; and, though it is unlikely that Argyrus touched the text, the Patriarch's dislike and distrust of Argyrus was such that he could not avoid the suspicion. After all, he reflected, the Pope was a prisoner. How was it that he had managed to send legates? What assurance was there that they represented his intentions? He refused to recognize their legatine authority. His caution was justified. On 15 April, a few days after the legates' arrival at Constantinople, Pope Leo died. By all the prece-

[1] Cerularius describes his suspicions in his letter to Peter of Antioch (coll. 784–5). He was shocked because Argyrus had kept back some money sent by the Emperor to be given to the Pope in order to pay his own troops.

dents of Canon Law legates cannot represent a dead Pope. When the news of Leo's death reached him, Cerularius could congratulate himself on his prudence. The legates now had no legal standing whatsoever.[1] In September Henry III appointed a new Pope, Victor II. But Victor was in Germany and did not come to Rome till the following April. He was not in touch with the legation, if indeed he knew of its existence.[2]

Though the Patriarch ignored the legates, they were well received by the Emperor. Encouraged by his cordiality they published the documents that they had brought with them. The report from Jerusalem was irrelevant, for no one at Constantinople had ever complained of the usages of the Church there. But the two draft replies to Leo of Ochrida's letter, which Humbert had caused to be translated into Greek, annoyed the Byzantines. A reply was at once published by a certain Nicetas Stethatus, a monk of Studium, the monastery that once had been such a devoted advocate of papal rights. It addressed the Roman Church in very courteous terms, but criticized its practices over unleavened bread and fasting on Saturdays, and added a further criticism of the ban on married priests and of its celebration of an ordinary and not a pre-sanctified mass during Lent. Stethatus's arguments are, it must be confessed, a little crude and his references to Holy Writ not always apposite. Humbert could easily have made an effective refutation. But instead, when he saw the treatise and had it translated into Latin, he lost his temper and issued a reply full of

[1] News of the Pope's death cannot have taken longer than two months to reach Constantinople. It is remarkable that Cerularius nowhere mentions his death except by implication. But it was his policy to involve the Papacy as little as possible, probably because he knew that any subsequent Pope would certainly endorse the Legate's actions. Leo had returned to Rome a few days before his death. (Watterich, *Pontificum Romanorum Vitae*, i, pp. 171 ff.)

[2] Pope Victor arrived in Rome on 3 April 1055. He disapproved of Leo's desire for an alliance with Byzantium and had not been consulted about his recent policy. See Jugie, op. cit., p. 199, n. 4.

screaming abuse. Stethatus, whose name he translated as Pectoratus, which, he says, means the beast that crawls on its belly, is told amongst other quips that he must have come not from a monastery but from a brothel. There was no attempt to answer the monk's criticisms; but Humbert ended with a counter-attack on certain Greek practices, such as the admixture of warm water with the communion-wine.[1]

Cerularius still held aloof. But the Emperor feared that Humbert's rage might endanger the political alliance that he desired. He forced Stethatus to retract his treatise and to come personally to apologize to the legates. Heartened by this success Humbert went further and raised the question of the *Filioque*.[2] He doubtless supposed that Pope Leo would have wished him to do so; for just before the legates left Italy the Pope had been allowed by the Normans to go to Bari and to give before a small local synod there his views about the desirability of the word.[3] Even under this provocation, which irritated the Byzantine public, Cerularius kept silent and ignored the presence of the legates. Humbert's patience was at last exhausted. On Saturday, 16 July 1054, just as the afternoon liturgy was about to be sung, he and his colleagues stalked into the Church of Saint Sophia and laid on the altar a Bull excommunicating Michael Cerularius, Leo of Ochrida, Michael Constantine, the Patriarchal Chancellor, and all their followers. They then strode out of the church, ceremoniously shaking its

[1] Stethatus's original treatise is published in Michel, op. cit. ii, pp. 322–42, a better edition than that published in Demetracopoulos, *Bibliothèque ecclésiastique*, i, pp. 18–36. Humbert's translation is given both in *M.P.L.*, vol. cxliii, coll. 973–83, and in *M.P.G.*, vol. cxx, coll. 1012–22, and his reply, *Contra Nicetam*, in *M.P.L.*, vol. cxliii, coll. 983–5.

[2] Humbert's memorandum, written, he says, at the request of the Emperor, is given in Michel, op. cit. i, pp. 97–111.

[3] Humbert refers to this council in his memorandum mentioned above. It is otherwise unknown, except that Anselm seems to have used some of the arguments put forward by Leo IX on this occasion in his treatise *De Spiritus Sancti Processione*. See below, p. 77.

dust off their feet. A deacon ran out after them and begged them to take back the Bull. They refused; and he dropped it in the street. It was picked up and eventually brought to Cerularius. When it had been translated for him he must have smiled; for few important documents have been so full of demonstrable errors. It is indeed extraordinary that a man of Humbert's learning could have penned so lamentable a manifesto. It began by refusing to Cerularius, both personally and as Bishop of Constantinople, the title of Patriarch. It declared that there was nothing to be said against the citizens of the Empire or of Constantinople, but that all those who supported Cerularius were guilty of simony (which, as Humbert well knew, was the dominant vice at the time of his own Church), of encouraging castration (a practice that was also followed at Rome), of insisting on rebaptizing Latins (which, at that time, was untrue), of allowing priests to marry (which was incorrect; a married man could become a priest but no one who was already ordained could marry), of baptizing women in labour, even if they were dying (a good Early Christian practice), of jettisoning the Mosaic Law (which was untrue), of refusing communion to men who had shaved their beards (which again was untrue, though the Greeks disapproved of shaven priests), and, finally, of omitting a clause in the Creed (which was the exact reverse of the truth). After such accusations complaints about the closing of the Latin churches at Constantinople and of disobedience to the Papacy lost their effect. The final *anathema maranatha* was followed by a statement that henceforward Cerularius and his supporters would be known as Prozymite heretics.[1]

Cerularius hurried to the Emperor with a Greek transla-

[1] The Bull of Excommunication is given in *M.P.L.*, vol. cxliii, coll. 1002–4, and the Greek translation, which is excellent, is printed together with the Patriarch's *Synodal Edict* in *M.P.G.*, vol. cxx, coll. 741–6. The translators were the Protospatharius Cosmas, Pyrus the Roman, and the monk John the Spaniard.

tion of the Bull. Constantine had just bidden a friendly good-bye to the legates, hoping that his plan for a political alliance had been achieved, and they had started out on their journey home. When he read the document the Emperor was profoundly shocked. But he was suspicious of Cerularius and did not at once agree that they should be summoned back to explain their behaviour. Instead, he sent a messenger, to ask them for the original Latin version of the Bull. The messenger caught up with them at Selymbria and returned with a copy of the text. When the Emperor found that the Patriarch's version was indeed correct he sent another message ordering the legates to come back and explain themselves before a synod at Constantinople. They refused and continued on their voyage.

Meanwhile the Patriarch's friends had caused the contents of the Bull to be known throughout Constantinople. The populace, which had already been annoyed by the arrogance of the Romans and resented the Emperor's cordiality towards them, flared up in demonstrations and riots. Constantine was alarmed and realized that public opinion backed the Church against him. He announced that he would punish the translators who had collaborated with the legates, and he arrested the relatives of Argyrus who were in Constantinople. He then ordered the offending Bull to be burnt. The riots were stilled. On Sunday, 24 July, a synod was held to record the whole business. It declared that irresponsible men had come from the West and had excommunicated the Patriarch and everyone who refused to conform with their doctrine about the Holy Ghost and their practices of shaving and of priestly celibacy. The text of the Bull and the Emperor's decree ordering it to be burnt were given in full. The letters that were brought by the legates were quoted and were pronounced to be the work of Argyrus. Humbert and his companions were then solemnly anathematized. The record was carefully drawn up so as not in any way to involve the Papacy nor the

Western Church in general. The scapegoats were the three legates and that worthy but unpopular official, Argyrus. The way was left open for any Pope who recognized that Humbert had acted *ultra vires* to resume friendly negotiations.[1]

The events of 1054 need to be studied in detail because the tradition has arisen that they mark the final breach between Rome and the Eastern Churches. In fact, though no Pope had been mentioned in the diptychs of Constantinople since 1009 and negotiations in 1024 to tidy up the position had failed, contact between Rome and Constantinople was not entirely broken. The political situation in Italy and the Patriarch's attack on certain Latin usages, due to his policy within his own patriarchate and to the Roman policy in Italy, had led to fresh negotiations which failed disastrously in 1054. But the failure did not necessarily compromise the Papacy, as the legates in 1054 had no legal standing. A subsequent Pope could have repudiated their actions without any loss of prestige. The situation was no worse than it had been in 1052, except for an increase in ill will. Why then has the episode been given such inflated importance? At Constantinople it was barely noticed at the time except as an internal crisis in which the Patriarch won a victory over the Emperor. But it was taken seriously in the West. Partly this was because the reform of the Papacy meant that events that concerned Rome were followed with keen interest throughout the Western Church. The sudden Greek attack on Latin usages thus soon received a wider and more hostile publicity than any previous piece of Byzantine polemics. Still more it was due to the personalities involved. Humbert was not in the least abashed by his mishandling of the affair. His own report reads like a hymn of triumph; and the West took him at his own value. Till his death in 1061 he remained the chief influence at the Curia. One of his fellow legates, Frederick of Lorraine, became

[1] Synodal Edict, loc. cit.; Jugie, op. cit., pp. 208–11.

Pope as Stephen IX. And Humbert's closest friend was Hildebrand, the future Pope Gregory VII. Rome therefore never dreamed of repudiating the legates' action but instead emphasized its righteousness, till at last it came to be believed in the West that the unprovoked attack of a contumacious bishop had been properly and legitimately punished by excommunication; and as neither the bishop nor his successors sought for absolution, they were henceforward in a state of schism. Humbert had been careful not to include the whole Church of Constantinople in his excommunication of its bishop; but as it continued to elect and support schismatic bishops, it too was schismatic.[1] This interpretation did not become fixed in Western minds for more than a century to come. By the fourteenth century the Greeks themselves believed that the schism had started under Cerularius, who was said to have replied to the papal attack by excommunicating the Pope and telling the Eastern Patriarchs to recognize him in future as senior Patriarch. It was probably the influence of the Western attacks on Cerularius that turned him thus into an Orthodox national hero.[2]

At the time the chief and most unfortunate outcome was

[1] Boso's Life of Leo IX, in *Liber Pontificalis*, ed. Duchesne, ii, p. 355, speaks as though the mission of 1054 had been amiably received and highly successful. He mentions the Emperor 'Monacham' but not the Patriarch. But Wibert's Life, in *M.P.L.*, vol. cxliii, coll. 498–9, reports with satisfaction the excommunication of Cerularius, and this, combined with Humbert's report, which was widely circulated, led to a general belief that the Byzantine Church had now been condemned for schism. See, for example, Sigebert of Gembloux, *Chronicon*, *M.G.H.Ss.*, vol. vi, pp. 359–60 (*ad ann.* 1054), and Annalista Saxo, ibid., p. 689 (incorrectly *ad ann.* 1051), both laudatory accounts of Humbert's excommunication of the Greeks. A Dominican treatise written at Constantinople in 1252 calls Photius the founder of the schism and 'Circularios' his chief successor as rebel against the Pope. Dvornik, *The Photian Schism*, p. 348.

[2] For Psellus's view on the events of 1054 see below, pp. 67–68. The rehabilitation of Cerularius, to which Psellus contributed, resulted in him being regarded as a saint and in a gradual exaggeration of the importance of his actions against the Latins.

the growth of bitterness on both sides. Soon after the legates' departure a pamphlet was published in Constantinople entitled *Against the Franks*. It is a deplorable piece of work; it cites twenty-eight Latin malpractices, some of which were authentic, but others were fantastic and obviously untrue. Cerularius may have inspired it; but it is unlikely that he really believed that the Latins ate the flesh of wolves or baptized infants with saliva. The pamphlet was almost certainly intended for internal circulation, and was an attempt by the Patriarch's friends to follow up his victory over the Emperor by listing the horrible errors that the Emperor had apparently been ready to condone. Its aim was to outrage semi-educated opinion at Constantinople.[1]

More serious were the Patriarch's efforts to secure the support of his Eastern colleagues. Immediately after the legates had departed he wrote a brief account of their visit to Peter, Patriarch of Antioch, who was a friend of his and, like him, a subject of the Emperor. It was a tendentious letter which implied that the whole Orthodox Church had been excommunicated. A little later he wrote more fully and accurately about the episode; and he added a list of Western beliefs and customs that he considered wrong. His main objections were against the use of the *Filioque* and unleavened bread; but he cited other irregularities, some of which were trivial and others imagined. He accused the Latins of rejecting the cult of relics; which was demonstrably untrue, in view of the eagerness with which Western pilgrims sought relics in the East and the prices which they were prepared to pay. He also said that they rejected the cult of images, perhaps because he had somehow learnt that the divines at the Carolingian Court had held Iconoclastic opinions. He added, quite erroneously, that they did not regard Gregory the Theologian, Basil the Great, or John Chrysostom as saints. This was perhaps based on

[1] The pamphlet is edited in Hergenröther, *Monumenta Graeca ad Photium Pertinentia*, pp. 62–71.

some debate when a Greek had cited these saints as supporting the use of leavened bread and the Latins refused to accept such arguments as final. Such beliefs, he declared, were rank heresy; how could the Faithful remain in communion with such people? He went on to say that no Pope had been commemorated at Constantinople since Vigilius, a statement which Peter hastened to point out was untrue; and he regretted that the Eastern Patriarchs still continued to commemorate the Popes. He then asked Peter to find out for him whether it was true that azymite practices were permitted at Jerusalem and Alexandria. Peter's answer to the question has not survived. But in fact, though the native Orthodox congregations in Egypt and Palestine used leavened bread, there were large Latin colonies of clerics and pilgrims at Jerusalem and of merchants with their chaplains at Alexandria, and in their chapels the Western practice was followed.[1]

Peter of Antioch's response to his brother of Constantinople was not entirely sympathetic;[2] but Cerularius soon had too many troubles of his own to start a controversy. He remained the dominant figure in the State till Constantine IX died the following January. Constantine's successor was his sister-in-law Theodora, an elderly virgin who was the last of the great Macedonian dynasty and whose popularity in Constantinople outshone the Patriarch's. When he tried to dictate to her as he had done to Constantine, she tartly told him to mind his own business and keep to Church affairs. She only reigned for eighteen months. Her successor, Michael VI, tried to copy her, but he was a weak old man; and Cerularius had no hesitation in plotting against him and using the influence of the Church to dethrone him in favour of the commander-in-chief, Isaac Comnenus. But when, counting on Isaac's subservient

[1] Michael Cerularius, letter 6 to Peter of Antioch, *M.P.G.*, vol. cxx, coll. 781–96.

[2] For Peter's reply see below, pp. 65–66.

gratitude, he began to meddle again in civil affairs and even to wear the purple buskins that were the symbol of Imperial rank, his popularity waned at Constantinople, where no one was ready to tolerate a Patriarch who saw himself as Emperor. Isaac, secure in the support of the army, quietly deposed him. He did not long survive his disgrace, but died in 1058. He does not deserve all the obloquy heaped on him as chief architect of the Schism. At least equal blame for the events of 1054 must be assigned to Cardinal Humbert. But the career of neither of them had been helpful to the cause of Christian amity.[1]

[1] For the later history of Cerularius see Bury, *Selected Essays*, pp. 198, 202, 213–14 ('Roman Emperors from Basil II to Isaac Comnenos'); Amann, art. cit., coll. 1678–80; Hussey, *Church and Learning in the Byzantine Empire*, pp. 155–6. That Cerularius was not as happy about the events of 1054 as his letters to Peter of Antioch might imply is suggested by Ibn Butlan, who found him distinctly worried when he saw him on July 20, four days after the legates had left the Bull in Saint Sophia. He was distressed at the breach, but may also have been anxious about the reaction at the Imperial Court. See Graf, loc. cit.

III

FROM 1054 TO THE FIRST CRUSADE

HOW small an effect was made at the time by the events of 1054 can be seen by the continuance of negotiations between the Eastern Empire and the Papacy. An understanding with Rome offered to the Emperor his only chance of retaining any influence in Italy. It had proved impossible to check the Norman advance. In 1071 the Norman leader, Robert Guiscard, completed his conquest of the southern half of the peninsula by the capture of the Byzantine capital, Bari. Soon afterwards he began to threaten the Balkan peninsula and Greece. The Empire was in no state to resist an invasion from the West; for a great military disaster at Manzikert in 1071 had thrown all Asia Minor open to the Seldjuk Turks. The gradual loss of the Anatolian provinces, on which the whole military organization of the Empire and much of its economic wealth were based, brought the administration near to chaos. In such circumstances no Emperor wished to add to his difficulties by making unnecessary enemies in the West. The Pope was the only potentate likely to be able to restrain the Normans; while the growing dependence of the Empire on foreign mercenaries, nearly all of them Latin, made it highly desirable for the Emperor to be on good terms with the Latin hierarchy, whatever the Patriarch of Constantinople might think.

But these same years saw a change in the position of the Papacy. At the beginning of the century it had been ineffectual and corrupt. The reforms undertaken by the German Emperors had restored its efficiency and its moral influence. The death of the Emperor Henry III in 1056 and the long minority of Henry IV freed the Pope from his

German shackles. The decree of 1059 placed papal elections entirely in the hands of the Roman Cardinals. The Bishop of Rome was no longer the petty creature of the Roman nobility or of monarchs from beyond the Alps, but an independent figure whose prestige was supreme in the West, and who must be treated with respect.

The fall of Cerularius from power under Theodora offered a chance for fresh negotiations. Argyrus was restored to favour; but it was too late for him to save Byzantine Italy, even though he sent an embassy to Germany to the dying Emperor Henry III to ask for help.[1] The Latin churches in Constantinople were reopened. We find Pope Victor II, Leo IX's successor, writing in the friendliest terms to the Empress to ask her to reduce the taxes on Western pilgrims visiting Jerusalem.[2] But Victor at the same time found it prudent to make a truce with the Normans.[3] Victor's successor Stephen IX, who as Frederick of

[1] Gay, *L'Italie méridionale*, pp. 508–9; Chalandon, *La Domination normande en Sicile*, i, p. 160.

[2] Letter in *M.P.L.*, vol. cxlix, coll. 961–2, attributed there to Victor III. Riant, *Inventaire critique des lettres historiques des Croisades*, pp. 50–53, suggests that the letter, which is addressed to 'Imperatrici A.', should be attributed to Victor II and that the recipient was the Empress-Regnant Theodora, 'A.' standing for 'Augusta'. Leib, *Rome, Kiev et Byzance*, p. 87 and n. 3, maintains that the writer was Victor III and the recipient Anna Dalassena, who was periodically regent for her son Alexius I when he was absent at the wars. In that case it must have been written in 1086–7. But the Emperor was at that time under a sentence of excommunication by the Papal Court, and it is unlikely that the Pope would have written then in such friendly terms to his mother. Moreover, the letter implies that a large number of pilgrims were regularly travelling to Palestine, which is true of 1055–6 but not of 1086–7, when the Norman wars and the Turkish invasions of Palestine had made pilgrimage difficult. The letter speaks of pilgrims visiting and praying at the Holy Sepulchre who had to pay taxes to Byzantine officials. It is possible that the Pope only means that taxes were levied on pilgrims on their way to Jerusalem, but in Theodora's time there may well have been Byzantine officials who charged pilgrims a tax for its upkeep, in the precincts of the Holy Sepulchre itself, which Constantine IX had recently repaired, having obtained the right to do so in a treaty with the Egyptian Caliphate.

[3] Gay, op. cit., p. 509.

Lorraine had accompanied Humbert on his disastrous legation, reverted to the policy of an alliance with Byzantium and, probably on the news of the deposition of Cerularius, nominated Desiderius, Abbot-elect of Monte Cassino, to lead a new mission to Constantinople. The legates had already reached Bari, in January 1058, when they heard that the Pope had died. Remembering what had happened in 1054 they prudently returned to Rome.[1]

In 1059 Pope Nicholas II signed a treaty with the Normans at Melfi. Guiscard was recognized as ruler of Apulia and Calabria and the Lombard principalities, which he was to hold under the suzerainty of the Holy See.[2] The settlement was a direct attack on Byzantine claims and caused resentment at Constantinople. In 1062 the Emperor Constantine X joined with the Empress-Regent of the West, Agnes, in an intrigue to elevate Cadalus, Bishop of Parma, to the Papacy in opposition to the legitimate Pope Alexander II. But Cadalus, who called himself Honorius II, was unable to maintain himself in Rome, and recognition was soon withdrawn from him.[3] The Byzantines had other troubles to occupy them. But Alexander II had been alarmed by the possibility of an alliance between Byzantium and Germany. He therefore took the opportunity of the accession of the Emperor Michael VII to send a congratulatory embassy to Constantinople in 1072 under Peter, Bishop of Anagni. Peter was instructed tactfully to raise the question of Church union.[4]

Unfortunately, Rome and Constantinople now had

[1] Leo of Ostia, *Chronica Monasterii Casinensis*, *M.G.H.Ss.*, vol. vii, pp. 702–3.

[2] For the Treaty of Melfi see Gay, op. cit., pp. 516–19; Chalandon, op. cit. i, pp. 170–2.

[3] Letter quoted by Benzo of Alba, *M.G.H.Ss.*, vol. ix, col. 622. See Dölger, *Regesten der Kaiserurkunden*, No. 952, ii, pp. 14–15. Constantine X is said to have recognized Cadalus (Honorius II) as 'Patriarch of Rome raised by Imperial authority over the universal Church'.

[4] Bruno of Segni, *Vita S. Petri Ananiensis*, *Aa.Ss.*, 3 August, p. 230.

different notions about the meaning of Church union. At Rome the dominant influence was that of Hildebrand, soon to become Pope Gregory VII; and he was gradually developing his theory that the spiritual power of the Papacy was to the lay power of emperors and kings as the sun is to the moon, and the lawyers of the Curia were beginning to fit this theory into legal and practical terms. It was not a concept likely to please the heir of Constantine the Great at Constantinople; and it demanded as a complement that the Pope's authority over all the Churches of Christendom should be unquestioned and complete. In the East, however, it was now generally held that the one supreme doctrinal authority in the Church was an Oecumenical Council at which every Church was represented, and that the government of the Church should be in the hands of the five historic Patriarchates, Rome, Constantinople, Alexandria, Antioch, and Jerusalem, with the Emperor enjoying a vague suzerainty as the Viceroy of God on earth. Thus to the Romans Church union meant the submission of the Eastern Churches to Rome, but to the Byzantines it meant that the Roman bishop should resume his place as the senior of the Patriarchs and be mentioned once more in the diptychs and be accorded all the deference and honorific titles due to him. It would be difficult to reconcile these views. Thus, when Alexander II's legate tried to open the question, the Patriarch, John Xiphilinus, backed by Michael Psellus, the Imperial Secretary, saw to it that the discussions were indefinitely postponed.[1]

In 1073 information reached Constantinople that Robert Guiscard was planning to invade the Balkans. The Emperor Michael, whose unreliable armies were fully occupied in fighting the Turks in Anatolia, decided that the new

[1] Bruno of Segni, loc. cit. As a result of an inspired dream the Emperor gave Peter a sum of money for the reconstruction of the Church of St. Magnus at Anagni. For the roles of Xiphilinus and Psellus, see Salaville, article 'Jean Xiphilin' in Vacant et Mangenot, *Dictionnaire de Théologie Catholique*, vol. xv. 2, coll. 3618–20.

Pope, Gregory VII, was the only man who could stop the Normans. An Imperial embassy went to Rome to offer Church union if Gregory would restrain Guiscard. The Pope fulfilled his part of the bargain. Guiscard was persuaded to make peace with Byzantium; and his daughter Helena was sent to Constantinople to be betrothed to the Emperor's son and heir. But when Gregory announced that he would come in person to the East with a large army which would beat back the infidel while he himself held a synod at Constantinople to settle all religious difficulties, the Byzantines were alarmed. The Patriarch John kept the negotiations spinning out till Gregory was distracted by problems nearer home.[1]

In 1078 Michael VII, a cultured but ineffectual Emperor, was dethroned in a palace-revolution and died soon afterwards. The new Emperor, Nicephorus Boteniates, imprisoned Michael's son and cancelled his marriage-contract with the Norman princess. Guiscard was furious; and soon afterwards he produced a Greek whom he had discovered at Rome, and said that he was the fallen Emperor. Gregory allowed himself to be convinced by the imposture. He authorized Guiscard to make war on the Empire in order to restore the pseudo-Michael; and he solemnly cxcommunicated the Emperor Nicephorus. For the first time for centuries there was a formal breach between the Papacy and the Imperial Court.[2] It was a grave tactical mistake.

[1] Anna Comnena, *Alexiad*, I. x, xii, ed. Leib, i, pp. 37, 43; Aimé, *Ystoire de li Normant*, ed. Delarc, p. 297. The marriage-contract between Constantine and Helena is published in Bezobrazov, 'Documents for the History of the Byzantine Empire' (in Russian), *Journal of the Ministry of Public Instruction*, vol. cclxv (1889), pp. 23–32.

[2] Anna Comnena, op. cit. I. xii, ed. Leib, i, pp. 43–47; Malaterra, *Historia Sicula*, *M.P.L.*, vol. cxlix, col. 1152; Jaffé, *Monumenta Gregoriana*, p. 330; Taccone Gallucci, *Regesti dei Pontifici Romani per le Chiese della Calabria*, No. XLI, p. 42 (circular to the bishops of southern Italy to inform them of the Emperor's excommunication); Jaffé, *Regesta*, No. 5210, i, p. 640 (forbidding the Venetians to ally themselves with an excommunicate).

Hitherto the Pope had always been able to play off the Emperor against the Patriarch. Now the two were forced into an alliance. The rupture was not accorded much attention in Byzantium because of the civil war that soon was raging there. But when in 1081 Alexius Comnenus secured the throne and restored order, the Pope committed the imprudence of excommunicating him also. The Normans had meanwhile begun their invasion of Epirus.[1]

Alexius Comnenus was the ablest statesman that Byzantium had produced for many generations. He was wise and indefatigable, genuinely pious, and passionately patriotic. He had been well educated and had cultivated tastes and wide learning. Personally he was kindly, tolerant, and generous, but he could be stern and even ruthless if it seemed to be his duty. As Emperor his one object was the welfare of the Empire; and, though his own standards of behaviour were strict, he was ready to countenance any ruse or intrigue that might benefit his people. In the prudent Byzantine tradition he preferred diplomacy to war, considering it less un-Christian, less expensive, and less destructive. He found both the civil service and the Church in a state of chaos and corruption; and he made it his business to reform them both. As the Lord's Anointed, he considered himself as the responsible authority over all ecclesiastical affairs. The Patriarch had to obey his orders; and he was ready to intervene over matters of faith, not to give decisions on doctrine, much as he loved theological debates, but to see that discipline was maintained and heresy checked. The new papal ideology was completely alien to his political theories. But he sincerely deplored the

[1] See Chalandon, *Essai sur le règne d'Alexis Comnène*, pp. 62–65. The excommunication of Alexius is not directly recorded but is clearly indicated by the Pope's *caveat* to the Venetians (see previous note) and by the negotiations for reconciliation (see below, pp. 61–62). In spite of the Norman war Alexius treated the Norman princess Helena with honour and eventually sent her to her uncle, Roger of Sicily (William of Apulia, *Gesta Roberti Wiskardi*, *M.G.H.Ss.*, vol. ix, pp. 153–5).

breach with Rome, not only for diplomatic reasons but from a real desire for Christian concord.

Gregory's sentence of excommunication shocked him and offended his people. In retaliation he closed the Latin churches at Constantinople, with the exception of those of the Venetians; for Venice was his ally in the Norman war.[1] He kept in touch with the Pope's arch-enemy, Henry IV of Germany; but he refused recognition to Henry's anti-Pope, Guibert of Ravenna, the self-styled Clement III, much to Guibert's surprise and disappointment.[2] Matters remained in this impasse till Gregory's death in 1085. Meanwhile the Norman invasion of Epirus had collapsed, while the Normans had shown their attitude to the Papacy by their sack of Rome.

The brief pontificate of Victor III did not change the situation. But in 1088 Odo of Lagéry became Pope as Urban II. Urban was a wise diplomat who saw that the Byzantine question had been mishandled. Alexius was now in a far stronger position than at his accession. He was secure upon the throne; the Normans had retired; he had driven back barbarian invasions from beyond the Danube; and he was holding the Turks. Urban understood that it was for the Papacy to make the first move towards a reconciliation. In 1089 he sent an embassy under Cardinal Rangier, or Roger, later Archbishop of Reggio, and Nicholas, Abbot of the Greco-Italian monastery of Grottaferrata, with a letter lifting the excommunication and asking the Emperor to reopen the Latin churches in his dominions and to allow them to use their own ritual. Alexius responded at once to this friendly tone. He summoned a synod to meet at Constantinople, which pronounced that the Popes' names had been omitted from the diptychs of Constantinople through carelessness and that it was uncanonical to remove them except by a decision of the synod. The

[1] Malaterra, op. cit., col. 1192.
[2] For Guibert's negotiations with Byzantium see below, p. 70 and n. 1.

Patriarch, Nicholas III, then wrote a letter to the Pope assuring him that the Latin churches were open once more and could employ what ritual they pleased. He promised that the Pope's name would certainly be inscribed in his diptychs, but proposed a delay of eighteen months, so that either the Pope could come himself to Constantinople to discuss the differences between the two Churches, or, if that were impossible, he could send a detailed treatise on these problems. A mild hint was added that the Pope should have sent a Systatic Letter on his accession; but his own presence or a full statement of faith would repair the omission. The Pope was then asked to extend his favour to certain Greek bishops in southern Italy. This was a tacit admission by the Patriarch that southern Italy had passed back to the See of Rome.[1]

Urban was satisfied by this answer. He tactfully overlooked the fact that the Patriarch addressed him as Brother and not as Father; and he must have known that he would never be able to visit Constantinople. Nor did he ever send the requested statement of his faith, probably because he did not wish to raise the question of the *Filioque*. In fact, he showed the Economy so dear to Byzantine churchmen. As no declaration of faith ever reached Constantinople his name was never added to the diptychs there. But all the same it could be said that any schism that there had been between the two Churches was closed. During the next decade there was an atmosphere of peace and friendship.

This goodwill was reflected in the chief polemical writings of the period. Even in the time of Cerularius many Eastern churchmen had deplored the idea of a breach within Christendom. Cerularius had been particularly anxious to have the support of his brother of Antioch. The Patriarch

[1] The important correspondence about these negotiations was discovered and published by Holtzmann, 'Unionsverhandlungen zwischen Kaiser Alexius I und Papst Urban II im Jahre 1089', in *Byzantinische Zeitschrift*, vol. xxviii (1928), pp. 38–67.

Peter III was an Antiochene by birth, who had been educated at Constantinople, where he had risen to be Grand Skevophylax of the Church of Saint Sophia. The Emperor Constantine IX had appointed him to Antioch in 1052, it was said on instructions given to him in a dream by the Mother of God herself. Cerularius received his declaration of faith in person, and performed his consecration. Once in Antioch Peter sent Systatic Letters not only to the Patriarchs of Alexandria and Jerusalem but also to the Pope. The letters to the Eastern Patriarchs contained the usual profession of faith and fraternal messages. The letter to Rome began with a preamble asking how it could be that the Church of Rome was no longer in touch with the Eastern Churches. Peter asked if there was any specific cause for separation. He recollected that Pope John XVIII had been mentioned in the diptychs of Constantinople; and he thought it most regrettable that 'the great successor of the great Peter' should hold himself apart from the divine fellowship of the other Churches and not take part in their fraternal discussions. He then made his own profession of faith, in which he passed with tactful vagueness over the question of the Procession of the Holy Ghost. The letter was entrusted to a Western pilgrim, who promised to give it into the hands of Argyrus in Italy; Argyrus was requested to pass it on to the Pope. In the meantime Peter added Pope Leo's name to the diptychs of Antioch.

Two years passed, and no answer came from Rome. But meanwhile, towards the end of 1053 Peter received a letter from Dominic, Patriarch of Grado, who was head of the Venetian Church and thus had many connexions with the East. Dominic wrote to complain of the difficulties that the Eastern Patriarchs put in the way of the Venetian chaplains in the East when they wished to celebrate the Sacrament with unleavened bread, and to remind the Patriarchs that he too bore the title of Patriarch. With his reply Peter enclosed a second letter from the Pope, which merely repeated his profession of faith; but to Dominic he sent a statement on his theory of ecclesiastical government. The Holy Oecumenical Councils had raised the number of Patriarchs to five; and there could not now be a sixth, any more than man could have a sixth sense. Peter could therefore only consider Dominic's title as honorary. As for the question of unleavened bread, he thought that the Pope was wrong to go against his four Eastern colleagues. That is to say, the Pope and the Patriarchs were on a level; and if unanimity was not possible, then the view of the majority should prevail. Peter reminded Dominic of Christ's promise to be present when two or three were gathered together in His name. Two or three minds were better than one.

The Pope at last replied in a letter drafted by Humbert. As might be expected it was a stern restatement of papal claims. Rome was the mother of all Churches and the Papal Court the supreme tribunal on earth. As the successor of Saint Peter the Bishop of Rome was perpetually infallible. The Patriarch of Antioch was then warned against evil influences in the East and against the encroachment of greedy neighbours. Peter was not favourably impressed by the letter. The See of Antioch, like that of Rome, had been founded by Saint Peter, as the Patriarch liked to remember; and there was always a certain resentment there when Rome claimed the exclusive heritage of the Apostle's powers. Moreover, Peter needed no warning against Cerularius, whom he knew well. The Patriarch of Constantinople had already (in 996) obtained the right, under the Emperor, to ordain his brother of Antioch; and Cerularius had tried to encroach further on Peter's prerogatives, when he had elevated a deacon of the Antiochene Church without reference to Peter, who had obliged him to apologize for it. Cerularius was also trying to control Armenian provinces that belonged properly to the Antiochene Patriarchate; and his whole policy of uniformity was distasteful and impracticable for the Antiochene Church, which included congregations still under Moslem domination, where a Syriac or an Arabic liturgy was in use.

When Cerularius wrote to Peter to tell him of the events of 1054, Peter sent him sympathy over the main issue and politely agreed, without much conviction, that Argyrus must have been the villain of the piece. But he could not refrain from criticizing many points in Cerularius's letter. He pointed out the falsity of the statement that no Pope had been commemorated at Constantinople since Vigilius and quoted the case of John XVIII. If within living memory a Pope had been mentioned on the diptychs at Constantinople, there was no reason why one should not be mentioned at Antioch. He then dealt with his colleague's complaints about Latin usages, and showed that some of Cerularius's charges were untrue, some were exaggerated, and nearly all were trivial. But he agreed about the undesirability of the use of unleavened bread. That savoured to him of Apollinarianism. Christ's body should be represented by a living substance, and the leaven symbolized life. But he recommended the use of Economy. Economy was still more necessary when it came to the controversy over the *Filioque*. Of course this was wrong; but, after all, he wrote, the Latins are our brothers, and it is only ignorance that makes them deviate. We must not demand from them the same scrupulous exactitude that we demand from our own highly educated circles. It should be enough that they confess the Mystery of the Trinity and the Incarnation. Perhaps, he suggested, they had lost the copies of the acts of the earlier councils.[1]

[1] Peter III of Antioch's correspondence with Constantinople, Grado, and Rome is given in *M.P.G.*, vol. cxx, coll. 752–820, and his Systatic Letters in Michel, *Humbert und Kerullarios*, ii, pp. 432–57. See also Michel, 'Die Botschaft Petros' III von Antiocheia an seine Stadt über seine Ernennung', *Byzantinische Zeitschrift*, vol. xxxviii (1938), pp. 116–18, and his 'Die römischen Angriffe auf Michael Kerullarios wegen Antiocheia', ibid., vol. xliv (1951), pp. 419–27. For the ordination rights

Peter of Antioch's attitude was probably that of most of the better educated Eastern ecclesiastics. The Latins were fellow Christians; and their divergences should be regarded with tolerant charity, so long as they did not attempt to force them upon others. But the Pope's claim to dictate to the Churches of the East was intolerable. The theory of the five Patriarchates was by now universally accepted in the East. To what extent this was an innovation is a matter of controversy; but it seems probable that ever since the fifth century, when the five Patriarchates were legally established, the doctrine had been held by the average Eastern Christian. It was certainly widely advocated at the time of the Iconoclastic controversy, though then it was directed against Constantinople. But hitherto the Pope, as *primus inter pares*, had generally been accorded special deference, and his views on doctrine had received more serious attention than those of the other Patriarchs. But the degradation of the Papacy during the tenth and early eleventh centuries had been ruinous for Roman prestige. Any advocates that there might have been in the East of Roman supremacy abandoned their theory as impracticable. Now, with startling suddenness, Rome revived her claims with greater vigour and precision than ever before. The East riposted by stating in equally clear terms the theory of the Pentarchy of Patriarchs.[1]

of Constantinople see Grumel, 'Les Patriarches grecs d'Antioche du nom de Jean', *Echos d'Orient*, vol. xxxii (1933), pp. 283–4, and for the contretemps over the deacon, Grumel, 'Le Patriarcat d'Antioche', *Echos d'Orient*, vol. xxxiii (1934), pp. 140–1. In one of his letters to Dominic of Grado Peter points out that strictly speaking only the holder of the See of Antioch is a Patriarch. The Bishops of Rome and Alexandria are Popes and those of Constantinople and Jerusalem Archbishops (*M.P.G.*, vol. cxx, col. 757).

[1] Nicholas III of Constantinople emphasizes the doctrine of the Pentarchy in a letter to Symeon of Jerusalem written about the time when he was negotiating with Pope Urban II. Grumel, 'Jérusalem entre Rome et Byzance: Une lettre inconnue du Patriarche de Constantinople à son collègue de Jérusalem', *Echos d'Orient*, vol. xxxviii (1939), pp. 104–17.

As yet neither in the East nor in the West did the general population concern itself with such theories. Latin pilgrims were always welcomed at Constantinople, though at the height of the Norman war in Italy certain restrictions were imposed by the Byzantine authorities, and towards the end of the century the Seldjuk invasions made travel difficult, and the number of pilgrims dropped. There were occasional complaints about the strictness of Imperial police officials; and whenever the frontier was closed because of disorders on the Moslem side, there was always an outcry from the Westerners whose journey was interrupted. But on the whole the pilgrims, whether they were humble folk or magnates, were kindly treated. There was sometimes trouble when they tried to steal relics that they could not purchase. The theft of the body of Saint Nicholas from Myra by citizens of Bari nearly caused fighting.[1] Other pilgrims received valuable gifts. When the Bishop of Langres pointedly and repeatedly expressed his admiration for the arm of Saint Mamas, which was preserved in the collection at the Imperial Palace at Constantinople, the Emperor Michael VII, somewhat reluctantly, presented it to him.[2] Meanwhile there were many Greek pilgrims who visited Rome where the tombs of Saint Peter and Saint Paul were a great attraction. When Guiscard was looking for a Greek to impersonate the fallen Emperor Michael he merely sent an agent to the shrine, knowing that he would soon find someone suitable there.[3]

There were also now many Latin residents at the Imperial Court, and religious problems were sometimes discussed there in a friendly spirit. Not many Byzantines yet took the dispute seriously. Psellus, the leading intellectual

[1] For the Translation of St. Nicholas see Leib, *Rome, Kiev et Byzance*, pp. 51–74.

[2] *Historia Translationis Sancti Mamentis, Aa.Ss.*, 17 August, pp. 444–5.

[3] Anna Comnena, op. cit. I. xii, ed. Leib, i, p. 45. For other instances of pilgrimages in both directions see Leib, *Rome, Kiev et Byzance*, pp. 84–99.

of the time, only mentions it twice in his surviving writings, once to state the theory of the Pentarchy and once, in his funeral oration on Cerularius, to praise the late Patriarch for his stand against the false doctrines of the Latins, in particular, their addition to the Creed.[1] He also had some part in discouraging Michael VII's negotiations with the Papacy. But when in Constantine X's reign a Georgian saint, George the Hagiorite, visited Constantinople, the Emperor received him in audience in front of a gathering where many Latins were present, and asked him what he thought on the question of the bread for the Sacrament. The saint's answer was full of tact. The Greeks, he said, were right to use leavened bread as an anti-Apollinarian symbol. The Greek Church had so often lapsed into heresy in the past that it had to be careful about symbols. The Roman Church, however, had never strayed from the path of Orthodoxy and therefore did not need to use the symbol of the leaven. The saint's biographer assures us that his words delighted the Latins who had never hitherto known how to defend their practice.[2]

Very little is known of the attitude of the Eastern Patriarchs apart from Peter of Antioch. His successor, Theodosius III, was a close friend of Cerularius, but seems to have taken no steps against the Latins. Indeed, we find him threatening to report the King of Georgia, of whom he disapproved, to the other four Patriarchs, which implies that he believed in an undivided Pentarchy of which Rome was a member.[3] Of the Church of Alexandria we only know the names of the Patriarchs; but it seems that they commemor-

[1] Michael Psellus, letter to Cerularius, in Sathas, *Μεσαιωνικὴ Βιβλιοθήκη*, vol. v, p. 509. Funeral Oration on Cerularius, ibid., vol. iv, pp. 348 ff. Relevant extracts are given in Michel, *Humbert und Kerullarios*, ii, pp. 476–81. See Dematrocopoulos, *Graecia Orthodoxa*, p. 8.

[2] Peeters, 'Vie de S. Georges l'Hagiorite', *Analecta Bollandiana*, vol. xxxvi–xxxvii (1917–19), pp. 137–8.

[3] Grumel, 'Le Patriarchat d'Antioche', *Echos d'Orient*, vol. xxxiii (1934), pp. 142–4.

ated the Pope in their diptychs at least till the middle of the eleventh century.[1] The Church of Jerusalem was in a special position. Byzantium was on excellent terms with the Fatimid Caliphs who controlled Palestine till the Seldjuk conquest. Romanus III had been granted by treaty the right to rebuild the Church of the Holy Sepulchre, burnt down by the mad Caliph Hakim, and Constantine X had carried out the work. In Theodora's time there were Byzantine officials attached to the church who collected tolls from the pilgrims for its upkeep. The Patriarch was invariably Greek by education if not by birth, and his chief churches used the Byzantine liturgy, though services in the villages were in Arabic. But Jerusalem was also in close touch with the West. The pilgrim traffic was at its height; and the Patriarch was unlikely to take any action that might offend his many visitors from the West and might decrease the number of gifts and endowments that they provided for his shrines. His jurisdiction was territorial and therefore included the several Latin establishments in Palestine. He could not enforce them to abandon their usages. It is probable that his diptychs continued to mention the Pope. Certainly none of the Latin pilgrims seem to have thought that there was any schism between the Patriarch of Jerusalem and themselves.[2] When towards the close of the century the Seldjuk invaders made life uncomfortable for the Patriarch, he would retire to Constantinople. But even so he kept a special relationship with the West. When the Emperor Alexius tried to negotiate a peace with the Normans in 1083 he chose Euthymius of Jerusalem to be mediator, knowing that the Normans would respect his rank.[3]

[1] Cerularius complained to Peter of Antioch that Alexandria still commemorated the Pope and that the Patriarch there permitted azymes, *M.P.G.*, vol. cxx, coll. 787–90. There is no other evidence of the Alexandrian attitude.

[2] See Michel, op. cit. ii, pp. 24–40. Michel finds no evidence of any breach between Jerusalem and Rome. See Every, *The Byzantine Patriarchate*, pp. 157–9.

[3] Dölger, *Regesten*, No. 1087, ii, p. 30.

The Russian Church depended upon that of Constantinople. By the middle of the eleventh century its head, the Metropolitan of Kiev, was a Greek appointed by the Constantinopolitan Patriarch. The arrangement suited the Russians, for had a Russian been appointed he would never have been able to keep aloof from the rivalries and intrigues that characterized Russian politics. The Russians therefore followed the ecclesiastical lead of Constantinople; but sometimes their bishops went further than the Patriarch, for the Emperor was not at hand to restrain them. John II, who became Metropolitan of Kiev in 1077, received some eight years later a letter from the anti-Pope Guibert of Ravenna, asking him for recognition and support. It seems that Guibert was disappointed not to be recognized at Constantinople and hoped that John might bring influence to bear in his favour. In his reply John addressed him as Pope, though he only called him 'most holy and venerable Brother'. Treating him as Pope, John went on to express his sorrow that the Holy See had diverged from the faith of the Seven Councils which in the past Rome had been the first to maintain. He referred to the unseemly use of unleavened bread, then to four incorrect practices over the Lenten Fast and baptism, which Photius and not Cerularius had condemned, and finally he mentioned the *Filioque*. Except over the azymite question he supported his views with arguments taken from Photius's works. He advised Guibert very strongly to send legates to Constantinople to announce his conformity with the correct practices. Throughout his letter his tone was friendly and sincere; and he apologized if what he had written seemed rude. But he had no doubts about his own righteousness.[1] But Guibert, when he made a *démarche* to Constantinople,

[1] Leib, op. cit., pp. 32–37, a full account, with references, of John of Kiev's correspondence with Guibert. The text of his letter is given in Pavlov, *Critical Essay on the History of Greco-Russian Polemic against the Latins* (in Russian), pp. 167–86.

did not follow his advice, and received no encouragement from there.[1] Shortly afterwards John was asked by one of his flock about the correct attitude of a Russian Christian towards a pagan, a Jew, and a Latin. With regard to the Latins, John declared that it was wrong to share the communion with azymites or with men who did not obey the canonical rules about fasting; but the faithful could join in the festivals of the Latins if to stay away would cause enmity or ill will; for that would be a greater evil. He did not approve of intermarriage with the azymites; for that was to share a sacrament with them. In particular, the Russian princes ought not to give their daughters to such men. Herein John went further than anyone as yet at Constantinople. He was clearly afraid of Latin political influence in Russia, which might be increased as a result of such marriages. This was a danger that had not arisen at Constantinople. The Russian royal line was of Scandinavian origin, and many Russian princesses had found Latin husbands. Indeed, Henry IV's Empress was a Russian. And, in spite of John, such alliances were continued. He seems to have assumed that a Latin princess married to a Russian prince conformed to her husband's faith and so raised no problem.[2]

The Emperor Alexius's reconciliation with Pope Urban II was not altogether popular at Constantinople, where Gregory VII's actions in excommunicating the Emperor and encouraging the Normans against the Empire had

[1] Guibert's letter to Basil of Reggio telling of his unfulfilled hopes of sympathy from Constantinople is given in Holtzmann, art. cit., pp. 59–60. Basil of Reggio seems to have sympathized with his case. See Basil's letter to the Patriarch, ibid., pp. 64–67.

[2] John's 'Canonic Answers to the Monk James' are published in Goetz, *Kirchenrechtliche und kulturgeschichtliche Denkmäler Altrusslands*, pp. 98 ff., and in Pavlov, 'Fragments of the Greek Text of the Metropolitan John's Canonical Answers', in *Additions, No. 22, to the Publications of the Russian Imperial Academy of Sciences*, No. 5 (in Russian). For later Russian statements see Golubinski, *History of the Russian Church* (in Russian), I. ii, pp. 820–8.

roused intense and lasting bitterness. But enlightened opinion supported the Emperor. About the year 1090 a deacon of Constantinople called Nicholas, who apparently hoped to obtain a bishopric in Bulgaria, wrote to the Archbishop of Ochrida, the head of the Bulgarian Church, to ask for a ruling on the errors of the Latins, which, in his opinion, were leading straight towards schism. The Archbishop was Theophylact, who was one of the most distinguished scholars of the time. He was a Greek from Euboea who had been the favourite pupil of Psellus at the University of Constantinople and had then been engaged as tutor to Michael VII's son Constantine. Unfortunately for him, his friend the Patriarch Nicholas III, who had a high regard for his abilities, appointed him to take over the administration of the Bulgarian Church. It was an important post, but it obliged him to move to a little town in the depths of Macedonia; and there he remained for the rest of his life, wistfully regretting the libraries and the lecture-rooms of the capital and writing innumerable letters to his many friends. Theophylact was shocked by the tone of the deacon's letter; and his long and careful reply recommended a more charitable attitude.[1] It is written in the intricate style fashionable at the time; but its argument is clearly stated. He enumerated the charges regularly made against the Latins: that they fasted at the wrong times, that they ate strangled meat, that their ceremonial at weddings and baptisms differed from the Greek. He could not regard them as serious errors. It seemed to him laughable that anyone should actually want to excommunicate the Latins because their priests shaved their beards and wore rings of gold and robes of many-coloured silk, or if they bent the knee instead of bowing to the altar. Nor was their insistence on priestly celibacy an unpardonable crime. If all these customs were based on genuine piety and there was a reciprocal tolerance over the

[1] Theophylact of Bulgaria, *De Iis in quibus Latini Accusantur*, *M.P.G.*, vol. cxxvi, coll. 221 ff.

divergences, what need was there to worry? Even with regard to their use of unleavened bread, there was nothing in the Scriptures nor in the Canons of the Seven Councils to forbid it. Theophylact believed the use of leavened bread to be symbolically more suitable; but it was a matter of tradition, not of any divine injunction. The practice of fasting on Saturdays was, he thought, unsupported by the Apostles or by the Fathers of the Church, but no one had denounced it as illicit. He went on to hint that some of the customs of his own compatriots could be called into question; and he wrote with bitter eloquence about the narrow and fault-finding attitude too often shown by the Byzantines, with their passion for criticizing others and their obstinate refusal to admit that they could ever possibly be wrong themselves.

There were, in his opinion, only two points in dispute which, if care were not taken, might lead to schism. One was the addition of the *Filioque* to the Nicene Creed. He thought that it was wrong and dangerous for the Latins on their own authority to have made an addition to a Creed that had been published by the Oecumenical Councils as the common symbol for all Christendom. Such an action was liable to cause divisions. He believed also that the addition was theologically incorrect, for reasons that he appended; but he scrupulously explained that his arguments represented his own personal view. Even here one ought not to be too critical. Much of the trouble was due, he maintained, to the poverty of the Latin language in theological terms. The one word *procedere* had to do the work of four Greek words, each of which had a different shade of meaning.[1] Latin theology was bound therefore to be a little cruder than Greek; and if the Latins chose to insert the word for their own internal exegetic purposes, there was

[1] Ibid., coll. 228–9. He says that *procedere* is the only word that the Latins have for the four Greek words *ἐκπορεύεσθαι*, *χεῖσθαι*, *διαδίδοσθαι*, and *προβάλλειν*.

no harm in it, so long as they remembered that the word did not occur in the Creed accepted by all Christendom. That is to say, so long as the Latins were not aggressive, charity, the Economy of the East, could be shown to their doctrines.

But would they refrain from aggression? Theophylact touches very lightly on the Pope's Petrine claims. In other works of his he shows himself perfectly willing to give the See of Rome its titular primacy. But here he makes it clear that he will not accept any doctrine or practice as being correct just because it has been pronounced as such from the papal throne, not even, he says, if the Pope declares that he speaks with the voice of Saint Peter and shakes the keys of the Kingdom in our faces. It was, he thought, an insult to Saint Peter to rely upon his authority in putting forward a doctrine that had not been endorsed by the councils of the Church, though all was well if the councils confirmed the papal propositions.[1]

It is clear that Theophylact did not consider the Churches of Rome and Constantinople to be in schism; nor did he see any reason why schism should develop, provided that neither Church interfered with the usages of the other, and provided, too, that the Papacy did not attempt to dictate to the Eastern Patriarchates. Unfortunately the second condition was unlikely to be realized, considering the temper of the reformed Papacy.

Theophylact's high reputation for learning and piety gave him considerable influence; and educated opinion at Constantinople, especially at the Imperial Court, seems to have shared his views. But among the clergy, even among the more moderate, there was some reluctance to be quite so tolerant about the use of unleavened bread, especially as the Latins were ready to plunge into controversy over it. A Latin called Laycus published an attack on the Eastern pro-zymite custom, which inspired the Patriarch of Jeru-

[1] Theophylact of Bulgaria, *De Iis in quibis Latini Accusantur*, *M.P.G.*, vol. cxxvi, col. 241.

salem, Symeon II, to take up his pen. Hitherto the Church of Jerusalem had kept out of the controversy; and Symeon was no enemy of the Latins. The welcome that he gave to their pilgrims was enshrined in Western tradition in the legend of his cordial interview with Peter the Hermit. But he lived in troubled times. During the reign of his predecessor Euthymius the Turks had taken Palestine from the Fatimids, and there had been some bitter fighting before the Turkish prince Ortoq restored order. The defeat of the Fatimids meant that Byzantium lost its favoured position at Jerusalem. About 1080 a rumour reached the monks of the Black Mountain that the Latins had taken over the chapel of Golgotha, which was reserved exclusively for their rights.[1] Meanwhile the Armenians increased their power in the Holy City; and they, like the Latins, employed unleavened bread.[2] The Patriarchate had tolerated divergent usages. But Laycus, who was probably an Amalfitan, seems to have had some connexion with the Latins in Jerusalem; and when his own practices were challenged in his own see, the Patriarch was forced to answer. Like Euthymius Symeon spent some years in Constantinople. He was there in 1086, but returned to Jerusalem before 1090. It was probably at Constantinople that he wrote his short treatise. It is mild and courteous in tone, and does not put forward any new argument. But Symeon makes it clear that he considers the use of unleavened bread to be completely wrong, and he does not wish to show charity towards it.[3]

[1] See Leib, op. cit., p. 29.

[2] It is significant that, unlike the Greek Patriarch, the Armenian Patriarch of Jerusalem did not think it necessary to leave the city till the actual beginning of the Crusaders' siege. Matthew of Edessa, *Chronique*, trans. E. Dulaurier, p. 225. The Egyptian vizier, al-Afdal, was a renegade Armenian who always favoured his former co-religionists.

[3] Symeon's treatise is published by Leib, 'Deux Inédits byzantins sur les Azymites au début du XII siècle', *Orientalia Christiana*, vol. ix, pp. 85–107. Leib doubted Symeon's authorship, as the treatise appears to answer one written by Bruno of Segni in about 1108. But Michel has shown that Bruno plagiarized an earlier treatise by a certain Laycus, whose

In the West Pope Urban's influence was all for peace and understanding. He avoided as far as possible raising any controversial issue, and he never made any direct reference to his claim of supremacy over the Eastern Churches. His friend, Anselm, Archbishop of Canterbury, to whom he left the controversy, took an attitude parallel to that of Theophylact. The bitterness that had been shown in the time of Cardinal Humbert seemed to be forgotten. In 1098 the Pope held a Council at Bari, in order to integrate the Greek churches of southern Italy and Sicily with the Latin churches of the province. There was little difficulty over matters of ritual. The Greeks were apparently to be allowed to retain their own liturgy and usages, even the use of leavened bread. But they raised a protest over the addition to the Creed, and the Pope's discourse on the subject did not satisfy them. Anselm, who was in exile from England, had accompanied Urban to the council, and at Urban's request he addressed the assembly. His speech was a model of reasonable and good-tempered argument. He understood that there was a slight difference between the Western and the Eastern conception of the Trinity; and he confined himself to the Western view, showing that procession from the Son fitted logically into it. It was not an innovation but a doctrine that was inherent in the Latin interpretation of the Creed. He assured the Greeks that the Latins venerated the original form of the Creed; and if they had added to it without consulting the Eastern Churches it was only because the word clarified a doctrinal point.[1] This was tantamount to saying that the Greeks need not add the word themselves to the Creed, but they must not say that it was wrong for others to do so. With that the Greeks were

work Symeon is answering. Michel, *Amalfi und Jerusalem im griechischen Kirchenstreit* (Orientalia Christiana Analecta, No. 121), pp. 34–47, giving the text of Laycus's work. Bruno's *De Azymis* is published in *M.P.L.*, vol. clxv.

[1] Hefele–Leclerc, *Histoire des Conciles*, v. 1, pp. 459–60. See Leib, *Rome, Kiev et Byzance*, pp. 287–94.

satisfied, especially as the council went on to canonize a Greek saint, Nicholas the Pilgrim.[1]

Soon afterwards Anselm was questioned by the Bishop of Naumberg about the errors of the Greeks. He sent back a letter which clearly stated his views. Like Theophylact he saw no reason why the divergences should lead to schism. The only difference that he took seriously was over the *Filioque*. He showed that the controversy there was really over the nature of the Trinity and that the Latins and Greeks held basically divergent views. He considered the Greek view to be wrong, and he thought that they had no right to object to the addition. But he did not regard the difference to be so great as to cause a breach. He emphatically regarded the Greeks as fellow Christians and not as schismatics. The treatise does not contain a single word that is discourteous to them. But he does not mention the question of papal supremacy.[2]

It is clear that at the close of the eleventh century neither at Rome nor at Constantinople did responsible circles believe that there was a schism between the Western and Eastern Churches. If the tact, the restraint, and the tolerance shown by the Pope and the Emperor and by the Archbishops of Ochrida and Canterbury could have been maintained and copied by their followers and successors, all might yet have been well. But, unfortunately, even before Anselm had written his treatise, the whole issue had been raised again in a more virulent form; and by a cruel irony it was the policy of the peace-maker Urban, which he intended to strengthen the concord between the Churches, that led to the worsening of relations and the ultimate breach.

[1] Barthelemy, *Vita S. Nicolai Pelegrini Tranensis*, *Aa.Ss.*, 2 June, i, p. 249.

[2] St. Anselm of Canterbury, *De Azymo et Fermento* (letter to Walram), *M.P.L.*, vol. clviii, coll. 541 ff., *De Fide Trinitatis*, ibid., coll. 259 ff., and *De Sancti Spiritus Processione*, ibid., coll. 285 ff.

IV

THE CHURCHES AND THE CRUSADES

AMONGST the motives that induced Pope Urban II to launch the great adventure which we call the Crusades, one of the strongest was his burning desire to help the Christians of the East. His contact with the Emperor Alexius kept him informed about the Turkish problem and the dangers that the Empire was undergoing. He heard from returned pilgrims that conditions were worsening along the pilgrim routes. In Jerusalem itself the death of Ortoq in 1091 and the succession of his quarrelsome sons led to the persecution of the Christians. The Patriarch Symeon was soon obliged to leave the Holy City with all his higher clergy and take refuge in the island of Cyprus. Urban thought that in the interest of all Christendom the West should come to the rescue of the East; and he hoped that if the East were rescued its gratitude would put an end to all the past ill-feeling, and that the Pope would thus be accepted without demur as the leader of Christendom.

In March 1095 Urban held a council at Piacenza, *contra schismaticos*, that is to say, against the anti-Pope Guibert and his supporter, King Henry IV of Germany. It so happened that two ambassadors from the Emperor Alexius were in Italy at the time. His wars against the Turks were going well, chiefly because of his subtle diplomacy; but he was desperately short of manpower, and he had sent these envoys westward to act as recruiting agents. When they heard that a council was being held at which prelates from all parts and many princes would be present, it seemed to them a suitable occasion for making the Emperor's need for recruits as widely known as possible. The Pope gave them permission to address the council; and they painted the problems of Eastern Christendom in such vivid colours that the Pope and his counsellors were convinced that nothing less than a whole army should be sent to the East; which was not at all what Alexius had desired.[1]

It was with this impression in his mind that Urban crossed the Alps and came at length to Clermont. There he held a council to settle the affairs of the French Church; and at the closing session, on Thursday, 27 November 1095, he preached his great sermon, summoning all Western Christendom to go to the Holy War. No authentic report of his actual words survives; but it seems that he began the speech by a declaration that Eastern Christendom had appealed for help, and it was the duty of the Western Christians to go to the aid of their brothers. The response was far more enthusiastic than he had ever expected. Within a year several great armies had set out for Constantinople; which, the Pope had decided, should be the meeting-place for the hosts.[2]

There are idealists who fondly believe that if only the peoples of the world could get to know each other there would be peace and goodwill for ever. This is a tragic delusion. It is indeed possible for men and women of education to enjoy the company and customs of foreigners and to feel sympathy for them. But simpler folk who find themselves in a country whose language and habits are unintelligible

[1] Bernold of Constance, *Chronicon*, *M.G.H.Ss.*, vol. v, p. 461; Hefele–Leclercq, *Histoire des Conciles*, v. 1, pp. 394–5; Runciman, *History of the Crusades*, i, pp. 104–5.

[2] Five chroniclers profess to give Urban's actual words. Each differs from the others, but all make him stress the need to help the Eastern Christians, who had appealed for help. The chroniclers are Fulcher of Chartres, *Gesta Francorum Iherusalem Peregrinantium*, I. iii, ed. Hagenmeyer, pp. 130–8; Robert the Monk, *Historia Hierosolymitana*, I. i–ii, *R.H.C.Occ.*, vol. iii, pp. 727–9; Baudri of Dol, *Historia Jerosolimitana*, *R.H.C.Occ.*, vol. iv, pp. 12–15; Guibert of Nogent, *Historia Hierosolymitana*, *R.H.C.Occ.*, vol. iv, pp. 137–40; and William of Malmesbury, *Gesta Regum*, ed. Stubbs, ii, pp. 393–8. See also Munro, 'The Speech of Pope Urban II at Clermont', *American Historical Review*, vol. xi (1906), pp. 231 ff., and Runciman, op. cit. i, pp. 106–8.

to them are apt to feel at a loss and resentful. So it was with the Crusader soldiers and pilgrims who passed in their thousands through the Byzantine Empire in 1096 and 1097. They had set out to rescue Eastern Christendom, but when they came to the land of the East Christians they found it strange and unwelcoming. The language was incomprehensible, the great cities unfamiliar and alarming. The churches looked different; the priests with their black beards and buns and black robes were quite unlike any Christian priests that they had seen before. Nor did the people seem glad to see their rescuers. They objected to the easy Western habit of helping yourself to what you wanted. Their peasants tried to hide away their possessions and stores of food; their merchants struck bargains that were not always generous nor even straight. There was a fierce gendarmerie that mercilessly attacked anyone who strayed from the road. The fact that it was their own behaviour that aroused enmity never struck the Western soldiers at all. The princes and prelates on the Crusade were better able to understand a foreign civilization. But, whereas the Pope's chief motive was the rescue of Eastern Christendom, the princes had other aims. Besides, the First Crusade was a loosely organized affair, and public opinion was very influential.

It was particularly unfortunate that the first Crusading army to enter Byzantine territory was the most unruly and disorganized. Peter the Hermit and Walter Sansavoir had no control over the hysterical peasants whom they led. Peter himself enjoyed a certain esteem among the Byzantine countryfolk. He possessed the qualities that they associated with saintliness. He was poor, ugly, and dirty, and rode upon a poor, ugly, and dirty ass. Several Balkan villagers joined his rabble, and many gave him alms. Even the Emperor was impressed by his personality. But his followers thieved and rioted at every stage of their journey. They were quite ungrateful for what was done for them.

They refused to take the advice given to them. When, entirely through their own greed and folly, they met with disaster at Civetot, they blamed the Emperor for it all.[1]

The armies led by the princes were not much better behaved; and most of the princes were truculent when the Emperor tried to institute disciplinary precautions. Godfrey of Lorraine's army sacked a suburb of Constantinople and had to be defeated in a battle by the walls before Godfrey would consent even to meet the Emperor. Bohemond the Norman's, though better disciplined, was allowed by him to pillage Castoria when the inhabitants refused to sell him all their foodstuffs and baggage-animals, and there was fighting with the Imperial gendarmerie at the crossing of the river Vardar. Raymond of Toulouse's troops kept straying from the road; and the papal legate himself, who was with them, was wounded by Petchenegs of the gendarmerie while doing so; but he bore no malice for the accident. Though the last of the armies to arrive, that of Robert of Normandy and Stephen of Blois, crossed through the Balkans without any untoward incident, already an atmosphere of mutual dislike between Crusaders and Byzantines had been created.[2]

The negotiations between the princes and the Emperor at Constantinople passed through some difficult moments but ended cordially enough. We do not know what part in them was played by the papal legate, Adhemar, Bishop of Le Puy, whom the average Crusader considered to be the supreme leader of the Crusade.[3] He was a friend of Urban's and enjoyed his confidence; and his policy was certainly that of his master. Soon after he arrived at Constantinople, a little late because of his accident, his chief friend among the princes, Raymond of Toulouse, veered round from ex-

[1] Runciman, op. cit. i, pp. 121–33.

[2] Ibid., pp. 134–71.

[3] 'The chief authority (in the army) is given to a bishop', i.e. Adhemar. Raymond of Aguilers, *Historia Francorum qui ceperunt Jerusalem*, xi, *R.H.C.Occ.*, vol. iii, p. 255.

treme suspicion of the Emperor to terms of close intimacy. But that may well have been caused by Alexius's tactful handling of the rivalry between Raymond and Bohemond. All the princes ultimately agreed to pay homage to the Emperor and to restore to him any lands that they conquered which had formed part of the Empire before the Turkish invasions. They had realized a fact that the West, both then and now, liked to overlook: that the Byzantine army was far stronger and more efficient than their own. They had to comply with his not unreasonable demands. But they did not realize what should have been obvious: that the Emperor's aims were not the same as theirs. The Crusaders had come to rescue Eastern Christendom, but they did not intend to become the mere mercenaries of the Empire. They were pilgrims too, and they wanted to press on to Jerusalem, the great goal of pilgrimage. Many of them planned to settle in the Holy Land, to ensure that it remained in Christian hands; and there were unashamed adventurers among them, seeking a lordship in the fabulous East. Moreover, they had come to fight the Holy War. Every infidel was their enemy.

The Emperor, however, considered that his first duty was to his own Empire, and his second duty to the Orthodox people of the East, who, though they might live under infidel domination, regarded him as head of the Christian commonwealth. To him the enemy was not the Moslems in general but those Turks who were threatening his Empire and persecuting the Orthodox; and if he could restrain the enemy by diplomacy rather than by warfare, so much the better. Alexius badly needed mercenaries, but only if they fought under his orders. A large independent army that might endanger his whole diplomacy by clumsy acts of aggression was not at all what he wanted. The idea of a Holy War was not acceptable to the Byzantines. Their stricter theologians, such as Saint Basil of Caesarea, maintained that war could never be holy, even if it might be necessary;[1] and Byzantium was particularly shocked by the sight of so many warrior-bishops and warrior-chaplains in the Crusading host.[2] But this point of view lay beyond the range of the Crusaders' understanding.

The villain of the story that follows was Bohemond of Taranto, the son of Robert Guiscard. He had fought against the Empire in his father's campaigns; and he bitterly resented the failure of the Norman invasion of Epirus a decade before. The south Italian throne had passed to his half-brother; and he was left with only a small vassal-principality there. He hoped to find a larger dominion at some strategic point in the East and so to help the Normans build up a Mediterranean Empire. He had tried to make the Emperor appoint him commander of the joint Byzantine and Crusader army; and the Emperor's refusal further embittered him.[3]

There was dissatisfaction over the first triumph of the Crusade, the capture of Nicaea. The town surrendered to the Emperor, who did not allow it to be pillaged and who treated his Turkish captives too kindly for Crusader tastes. The next triumph, the victory at Dorylaeum, was won with very little Byzantine help; and during the long march across Anatolia the Crusaders found fault with their Greek guides and the small Byzantine company which was with the army. Bohemond did all that he could to increase the

[1] St. Basil of Caesarea, letter No. 188, *M.P.G.*, vol. xxxii, col. 681.

[2] 'The Latins have not the same notion of a priest as we have. . . . The Latin barbarian celebrates the divine mysteries and at the same time girds a shield on his left arm and holds a lance in his right; while he gives communion with the divine Body and Blood, he watches carnage and becomes a man of blood himself.' Anna Comnena, *Alexiad*, x. viii, ed. Leib, ii, p. 218. Latin priests had in fact been forbidden to bear arms (Kirch, *Enchiridion Fontium Historiae ecclesiasticae antiquae*, Nos. 190, 638, 641, pp. 117–18, 401, 402, quoting Tertullian, the *Canones Apostolorum* of *c.* 400 and the Council of Toledo in 400). But the ban was not official and was generally disregarded. Even the saintly Adhemar, though he may not actually have worn armour, took an active part in battles and was himself largely responsible for the victory of Dorylaeum.

[3] Runciman, op. cit., pp. 163–4.

feeling of hostility. The crisis came over the capture of Antioch.

The story of the Crusaders' siege of Antioch and their own subsequent siege there is one of the great epics of history; and the Crusaders fought their battle alone, without any direct help from Byzantium. The Emperor had promised to come to their help and set out with his army. But it was a dangerous military undertaking; and when refugee Crusaders told him, falsely, that all was lost at Antioch, and he knew that a Turkish army was approaching to cut his communications, he retired, preferring not to risk the fate of his Empire. His strategy was prudent; but he made a great psychological mistake. The Crusaders felt that the Byzantines had deliberately let them down. By the treaty signed at Constantinople, Antioch should certainly have been restored to the Empire. But had not Alexius forfeited it by failing to come in person to take it over? When Bohemond, who had been responsible for the city's capture, claimed it for himself, public opinion in the army supported him, and he had his way, in spite of the protests of Raymond of Toulouse. But Bohemond himself was uncomfortable at having broken his oath. He later forged a secret treaty between himself and the Emperor which purported to have allotted him the city.[1]

A few months earlier Baldwin of Boulogne had seized another formerly Imperial city, Edessa or Urfa. Alexius condoned the seizure of Edessa. The population there was almost entirely Armenian and Syrian Jacobite; and it would have been difficult for him to keep open communications with so distant a post. But Antioch was a different matter. It was a city of great strategic importance, and its population was largely Greek. He was determined to

[1] Runciman, op. cit., pp. 174 ff. Krey, 'A Neglected Passage in the Gesta', in *The Crusades and other Historical Essays presented to D. C. Munro*, pp. 57–78, proves, I think convincingly, that Bohemond forged the passage referring to a secret treaty between him and Alexius.

recover control of it. There could be no real peace now between him and Bohemond.

The quarrel over Antioch was bound to spread into the religious field. At the outset of the Crusades the princes, even Bohemond, had been careful to remind their ignorant soldiers that the Greeks and the Syrian Orthodox were their brothers in Christ. Adhemar of Le Puy, no doubt following the Pope's instructions as well as his own large sympathies, eagerly sought the co-operation of the Eastern Churches. The Patriarch of Antioch, a Greek from Constantinople called John the Oxite, had refused to desert his people when the Crusaders approached and had stayed in the city during the siege. The Turks had treated him with cruelty, even hanging him over the walls in a cage. On the Crusaders' entry Adhemar hastened to restore him to his throne, while the Frankish chroniclers reported with admiration of his courage. In the great cathedral of Saint Peter, Latin services were held side by side with Greek.[1] When the Crusaders captured the town of Albara and founded a new bishopric there, the Latin bishop was, it seems, consecrated by John.[2] About the same time Adhemar made contact with the exiled Patriarch of Jerusalem, Symeon, who was still in Cyprus. Symeon hastened to send from the island foodstuffs and other goods of which the Crusade was in need; and his gifts were received with gratitude.[3] When Adhemar thought that it was time to send a report to the West from Antioch he wrote his letter in the name of 'Symeon, Patriarch of Jerusalem, and Adhemar, Bishop of Le Puy, and principally the latter, who was given charge of the Christian army by Pope Urban'.[4] A few months later he sent an urgent request to the West for more

[1] Albert of Aix, *Liber Christianae Expeditionis*, iv. 3, *R.H.C.Occ.*, vol. iv, p. 433, calling the Patriarch John 'virum Christianissimum'.

[2] *Anonymi Gesta Francorum*, x. 31, ed. Brehier, pp. 36–38.

[3] Albert of Aix, op. cit. vi. 39, p. 489.

[4] Letter of Adhemar in Hagenmeyer, *Die Kreuzzugsbriefe*, pp. 141–2.

recruits, and to make it more effective he wrote the letter in the name of the Patriarch alone. Adhemar certainly drafted the letter himself; and it is striking that Symeon is given the title of 'Apostolicus', a title which in the past Rome had grudged to the Patriarch of Jerusalem. He is made to speak as the head of all the bishops, both Greek and Latin, in the East, which was an infringement of the rights of his senior, the Patriarch of Antioch; and he threatens with excommunication anyone, in the West or in the East, who fails to fulfil his Crusading vow. It is a remarkable document for a papal legate to have written on behalf of an Eastern prelate. The Pope himself would not have used more superb language. But the implied neglect of the rights of the Patriarch of Antioch suggests that John of Antioch's relations with the Crusaders were worsening.[1]

On 1 August 1098 there occurred one of the greatest tragedies of the Crusades, the premature death of Adhemar of Le Puy.[2] It robbed the Crusaders not only of their one acknowledged leader but also of the one man who knew what was in the Pope's mind. The effect of his death was soon seen. On 11 September the princes met to send a letter to the Pope. In it they reported Adhemar's death, and they suggested that the Pope should come out himself to the East. He was the heir of Saint Peter; he should take over Saint Peter's other see, Antioch. It is hardly credible that they expected Urban to be able to leave Italy or that they thought that the patriarchates of Rome and Antioch could be combined. But it is significant that they completely ignored the existence of the legitimate Patriarch John. The

[1] Letter of Adhemar, in Hagenmeyer, *Die Kreuzzugsbriefe*, pp. 146–9. The Westerners seem by now generally to have believed the See of Jerusalem to be more important than that of Antioch. Some even considered that it should have the primacy amongst all the sees of Christendom. See the anonymous *Tractatus Eboracensis*, *M.G.H. Libelli de Lite*, vol. iii, p. 659.

[2] *Anonymi Gesta Francorum*, x. 30, p. 166; Raymond of Aguilers, op. cit. xiii, p. 262; Fulcher of Chartres, op. cit. I. xxviii, p. 258; Letter of the Princes, in Hagenmeyer, op. cit., p. 164.

same letter spoke of the difficulties that they had encountered from heretics, Greek, Armenian, Syrian (probably Nestorian), and Jacobite.[1] By Greek heretics the princes probably meant Greek-speaking Paulicians, who certainly existed in the neighbourhood of Antioch.[2] But the wording was ominous. Symeon of Jerusalem, watching from Cyprus, must have wondered about his future rights. He was never to know. He died in Cyprus a few days before the Crusaders entered into Jerusalem, in July 1099.[3]

The Crusaders found at Jerusalem neither a Patriarch nor the higher clergy of the Patriarchate. Symeon was dead, and his bishops were still in exile. It seemed perfectly reasonable for the Latins to elect a Patriarch from amongst their own bishops. No one bothered to consider the canonicity of the appointment, dubious though it was; and in the absence of the Greek bishops and a Greek candidate, the Orthodox throughout Palestine accepted the Latin candidate without demur. It must be remembered that to many of the Syrian Orthodox the Greeks who had controlled their Church had been almost as foreign as the Franks. Unfortunately the first Latin Patriarch, Arnold of Choques, began his reign by trying to eject the various heretic sects from their chapels in the church of the Holy Sepulchre and by torturing Orthodox monks to make them reveal where they had hidden the True Cross and other relics when Symeon fled to Cyprus.[4] Daimbert of Pisa, who replaced Arnold a few months later, went further. He tried to reserve the Holy Sepulchre solely for Latin services and to eject all native Christians, even the Orthodox, from their establishments

[1] Letter of the Princes, loc. cit.

[2] The Crusaders had already encountered a Paulician settlement near Antioch. *Anonymi Gesta Francorum*, iv. 11, p. 62.

[3] Albert of Aix, op. cit. vi. 29, p. 489.

[4] Raymond of Aguilers, op. cit. xxi, p. 302; Fulcher of Chartres, op. cit. I. xxx, pp. 309–10; William of Tyre, *Historia rerum in partibus transmarinis gestarum*, ix. 4, *R.H.C.Occ.*, vol. i, p. 369.

in or near Jerusalem; and he shocked Oriental propriety by introducing canonesses to serve at the Sepulchre.[1] God took His revenge by refusing to perform the accustomed miracle of the Holy Fire on Easter Saturday, 1101, till the Orientals were invited to participate; and King Baldwin I saw to it that the native Christians recovered their rights.[2] Henceforward, till Saladin captured Jerusalem in 1187, the Orthodox in Palestine submitted willingly to the Latin hierarchy. The account of the Russian pilgrim, Daniel of Tchernigov, who visited the Holy Places in 1106/7 is very instructive. He was made equally welcome at Greek and Latin monasteries. He was shown particular favour by King Baldwin I. At the ceremony of the Holy Fire he saw Greek and Latin clerics working in harmony, though he noted with interest that while the Greek lamps in the Tomb were lit miraculously, the Latin lamps had to be lit from them. It appears from his narrative that the leading Greek ecclesiastic left in Palestine, the Abbot of Saint Sabas, to whom the king paid especial deference, was on this occasion in charge of the Sepulchre.[3]

It is possible that the Latin ecclesiastics in Palestine would have liked to implement Daimbert's policy of enforcing conformity. Throughout the duration of the Latin kingdom every Patriarch without exception was a man who had been born and brought up in the West, and none of them had any sympathy for the Orientals. But the Crown protected the natives, and was always anxious to keep the Patriarchate under control. It should be remembered that of the five queen-consorts of Jerusalem during the twelfth century only one, the queen-dowager of Sicily whose marriage was soon annulled, was not born an Orthodox princess. The queens of Baldwin I and Baldwin II were Ar-

[1] Fulcher of Chartres, op. cit. III. iii, pp. 368–9; Matthew of Edessa, *Chronique*, II. clxx, trans. Dulaurier, pp. 233–4.

[2] Fulcher of Chartres, op. cit. II. viii, p. 396.

[3] Daniel the Higumene, *Vie et Pèlerinage*, trans. de Khitrowo, *Itinéraires russes en Orient*, pp. 75–83.

menians of the Orthodox rite; the queens of Baldwin III and Amalric I were Byzantine princesses.[1] We find Queen Melisende, Baldwin II's daughter, giving handsome endowments to the Abbey of Saint Sabas. She also, with admirable impartiality, patronized the Syrian Jacobites.[2] In 1169 the Byzantine Emperor Manuel joined with the local Latin authorities to undertake repairs to the chief shrines. He sent artists in mosaic to decorate the Church of the Nativity at Bethlehem where Eastern and Western saints were both depicted; and the same artists worked in the Holy Sepulchre and the chapel of the Dormition on Mount Sion. Greek canons served at the Holy Sepulchre.[3] There was certainly no schism between the Greek and Latin Churches in Palestine. It is only towards the end of the century that a slightly discordant note appears. The Greek John Phocas, who made a pilgrimage to Jerusalem in 1184 and in general was not dissatisfied with his reception and spoke with approval of the Latin Bishop of Bethlehem for displaying a portrait of the Emperor Manuel, reports with glee the fiasco of a miracle attempted by a Latin prelate whom he calls the 'intruder' Bishop of Lydda.[4] It may be that the Latin Patriarch Heraclius, a corrupt and intolerant man who particularly disliked the Byzantine-born Queen-Dowager Maria, was showing some hostility

[1] The native Christians exercised further influence in Frankish households through doctors and grooms, who came usually from the local Orthodox community, such as Suleiman ibn Daoud and his elder son, who were Court physicians under Amalric I, and his younger son, who was Court riding-master. See Cahen, 'Indigènes et Croisés', *Syria*, vol. xv (1934), pp. 351–60.

[2] Röhricht, *Regesta Regni Hierosolymitani*, pp. 106–7. For Melisende's relations with the Jacobites, see Nau, 'Le Croisé lorrain Godefroy d'Ascha', *Journal asiatique*, IX, vol. xiv (1899), pp. 421–31.

[3] See Runciman, op. cit. iii, pp. 379–81. For the presence of Greek canons at the Holy Sepulchre, see Rozière, *Cartulaire du Saint-Sépulcre*, p. 177.

[4] John Phocas, *A Brief Description*, trans. Stewart (Palestine Pilgrims' Text Society), pp. 31, 34.

towards the Orthodox, who began to sigh again for the Greek hierarchy.[1]

There was, however, another latent source of discord. The traditions of the Orthodox Patriarchate of Jerusalem give the names of seven or eight Greek Patriarchs covering the period from 1099 to 1187.[2] One might have supposed that they were a later invention of Orthodox extremists who hated to admit that the Latin line had ever been recognized, were it not that there was a Greek Patriarch ready to step into the breach when Saladin expelled the Latin hierarchy in 1187,[3] and were it not that the names of two of them appear in contemporary sources. A diptych, dated about 1166, kept at the Monastery of Saint Catherine on Mount Sinai, commemorates John and Nicephorus, Patriarchs of Jerusalem.[4] John, Patriarch of Jerusalem, attended a council at Constantinople in 1157 and Nicephorus one in 1166; and John published a little pamphlet against Latin usages about

[1] Heraclius was elected Patriarch against the wishes of the local Franks, led by William of Tyre, whose policy was good relations with the local communities. William of Tyre, op. cit. xxii. 4, p. 1068; Ernoul (*Chronique d'Ernoul et de Bernard le Trésorier*), ed. Mas Latrie, pp. 82–84.

[2] The list given by Le Quien, *Oriens Christianus*, iii, pp. 498–503, based on that in Dositheus, *Ἱστορία περὶ τῶν ἐν Ἱεροσολύμοις Πατριαρχευσάντων*, ii, p. 1243, which follows the traditions of the Patriarchate, gives eight names between Symeon II and Athanasius II, the Patriarch who, according to Dositheus, returned to Jerusalem in 1187. They are: Agapius I, Sabas, Eucherius I, Macarius III, Jacobus II, Arsenius II, Johannes VII or Nicholaus, and Nicephorus II. Le Quien queries Agapius, Eucherius, and Macarius.

[3] Though Athanasius II seems to have gone to Jerusalem in 1187, we find the Patriarch Dositheus of Jerusalem in Constantinople in 1191 (Nicetas Choniates, *Historia*, Bonn edition, p. 529). It seems likely that the Emperor had adopted the habit of nominating to the See of Jerusalem during the later years of its exile. In 1191 the Patriarch Leontius had just died, and Dositheus had probably been appointed in Constantinople and had not yet gone to his see. He was of Venetian origin.

[4] This diptych is published in Brightman, *Liturgies Eastern and Western*, i, pp. lii, 500–2. It commemorates as living Nicephorus of Jerusalem, Luke of Constantinople, Sophronius of Alexandria, and Athanasius of Antioch. This dates it at roughly 1166. It mentions John as a recent Patriarch of Jerusalem.

the year 1160.[1] It seems likely that when Symeon died in Cyprus in 1099, the Greek bishops from Palestine who were with him there took it upon themselves to elect a successor. They could argue that they were legally justified; and, though they could not return to Palestine themselves, they regarded the Latin hierarchy set up there as intrusive. They stayed on in Cyprus, out of touch with their former flocks, who had accepted the Latins. The Fatimids of Egypt, who controlled the Sinai peninsula, did not wish any of their subjects to recognize Latin superiors; so the Abbot of Saint Catherine's, who, *ex officio*, possessed an Egyptian bishopric, and much of whose revenues came from Egypt, therefore recognized the Greek line; and probably the Church of Alexandria did the same. The Emperor at Constantinople was more realistic. He did not press the claims of the exiled hierarchy but kept it in reserve till it might be useful. About 1150 the Emperor Manuel, with the situation at Antioch in mind, thought it worth while to remind the world that there was an alternative line of Patriarchs for Jerusalem and brought the claimant to Constantinople. By 1167 his relations with the King of Jerusalem had greatly improved; and the Greek Patriarch was pushed tactfully into the background again, to re-emerge in 1187.[2]

It was at Antioch, not at Jerusalem, that trouble started. Once that Adhemar was dead and Bohemond was established as Prince of Antioch, the Patriarch John's position became impossible. Bohemond knew that the Emperor intended to regain possession of the city and that the Greeks

[1] Chalandon, *Les Comnène, Jean II Comnène et Manuel I Comnène*, pp. 642, 648, 651, 653; Krumbacher, *Geschichte der byzantinischen Litteratur*, p. 91.

[2] The wedding-ceremony at Constantinople in December 1161 of the Emperor Manuel and Maria of Antioch was conducted by the Patriarchs Luke of Constantinople, Sophronius of Alexandria, and Athanasius of Antioch (Cinnamus, *Epitome Historiarum*, Bonn edition, pp. 210–11). If a Patriarch of Jerusalem whom the Emperor recognized had been in Constantinople at the time it seems likely that he too would have assisted.

there and their Patriarch would certainly support him. He treated John with discourtesy and suspicion. When, in 1099, Latin bishops were appointed for Tarsus, Artah, Mamistra, and Edessa, the candidates travelled to Jerusalem to be consecrated by the Patriarch Daimbert, in contravention of John's rights. In 1100 John left Antioch and retired to Constantinople, together with his upper clergy. The official Latin version, designed to preserve the apostolic succession, was that he saw that as a Greek he could not conveniently preside over Latins and so resigned his see. But he himself thought otherwise. He had been driven into exile. Soon after his arrival at Constantinople he resigned, anxious to recover from his bitter experiences in the peace of a monastery, where he penned an unfriendly treatise against the azymites. His exiled clergy, with the Emperor's approval, appointed a successor, whom the whole Orthodox world regarded as the legitimate Patriarch. The Greeks in the principality might be forced to submit to a Latin hierarchy, but they openly desired the return of the Greek line; and it became a fundamental point in Imperial policy to have the See of Antioch restored to Orthodoxy.[1]

One can therefore say that a schism started in Antioch in 1100, with two rival lines of Patriarchs, each claiming to be in the apostolic succession. Rome and the Latins supported the hierarchy in possession of the see, and Constantinople and the Greeks the hierarchy in exile. This schism at Antioch was a prime cause of the general schism between the Eastern and Western Churches.

Relations between the Emperor Alexius and the Franks worsened for several reasons. The three Crusades of 1101 all met with disaster in Anatolia; and the blame for the dis-

[1] For John the Oxite see Grumel, 'Les Patriarches d'Antioche du nom de Jean', *Echos d'Orient*, vol. xxxii (1933), pp. 286 ff. John himself certainly considered that he had resigned only on his arrival at Constantinople. His act of abdication survives, given in Benechewitch, *Catalogus Codicum Manuscriptorum Graecorum Siniaticorum*, p. 279. The official Latin view is given by William of Tyre, op. cit., pp. 273–5.

asters was laid on the Emperor by the Crusaders, especially by the Lombards, whose catastrophe was mainly due to their refusal to take the Emperor's advice. The chief reason for the Crusaders' suspicion of Alexius was his continued diplomatic dealings with the Turks. Their resentment was increased when they captured from the Egyptians copies of a correspondence between the Emperor and the Fatimid Caliph, in which the former repudiated any connexion with the Frankish invasion of Palestine. The fact that the Emperor's generosity and his good relations with the Fatimids enabled him to redeem large numbers of Frankish captives held in Egypt was brushed aside. In 1102 King Baldwin I wrote to him to complain that he had been unhelpful to the Crusaders of 1101, and entrusted the letter to a bishop called Manasses, who was to call at Constantinople on his way from Palestine to Italy. Alexius tried to explain to Manasses that Baldwin had been misinformed and that he on his side had his grievances. He asked Manasses to report his point of view to the Pope.

Pope Paschal II, Urban's successor, was a weak, touchy man, with none of his predecessor's sagacity. When Manasses, who had not liked either the Emperor or the Byzantines, gave a garbled and unfriendly version of the Imperial message, Paschal was roused to fury. Alexius received neither redress nor sympathy.[1]

In 1102, while Bohemond was held in captivity by the Danishmend Turks, his nephew and regent, Tancred, annexed the last Byzantine possession in Syria, Lattakieh. Two years later the Byzantine fleet sailed eastward and recaptured Lattakieh and various Cilician ports occupied by the Normans. Bohemond, who had just been released, decided to return to Italy deliberately to seek for help against

[1] Albert of Aix, op. cit. viii. 41, 47–48, pp. 582, 584–5. Albert calls Manasses's see 'Barzenona' or 'Barcinona'. It was certainly not Barcelona, whose archbishop at the time was Berengar II. I have not been able to identify it.

Byzantium. He found the Pope already prejudiced by Bishop Manasses against the Emperor. It was easy for Bohemond to convince him that Byzantium was blocking the whole Holy War. When Bohemond travelled on to France he was accompanied by a papal legate, Bruno of Segni, who was to help him to organize a Crusade against Byzantium.[1]

If the expulsion of the Patriarch John from Antioch was the first turning-point in the general schism, Paschal's support of Bohemond was the second and the more dangerous. The Byzantines had been shocked by Gregory VII's excommunication of the Emperor. But it had been soon lifted; and the Emperor was a man and fallible. His excommunication did not involve the excommunication of all his subjects. But to preach a Holy War against the Empire, the Orthodox Roman Empire, could only mean that the Pope regarded all its citizens as being no better than the infidel. By any reckoning this was a declaration of schism. Fortunately for Christendom this Holy War was a fiasco. Bohemond crossed into Epirus in October 1107, accompanied by a papal representative; but after eleven miserable months he was forced to surrender to the Emperor. According to a treaty signed in the Emperor's camp by the river Devol, with the papal representative as witness, Bohemond was to retain the Principality of Antioch, but as a vassal to the Emperor, to whom and to whose heir he swore allegiance; and he agreed that the Patriarchate of Antioch should be restored to the Greek line. In fact, the Treaty of Devol remained a dead letter; for Antioch was now held by Tancred, who had no intention of becoming a vassal to Byzantium or of admitting a Greek Patriarch. He repudiated his uncle's signature and soon reoccupied the Byzantine seaports in Syria and Cilicia. But henceforward the Emperor

[1] Ordericus Vitalis, *Historia Ecclesiastica*, xi, ed. Prévost, iv, pp. 210–13; William of Tyre, op. cit. xi. 1, p. 450; Anna Comnena, op. cit. xii. 1, vol. iii, p. 53.

could invoke a treaty witnessed by a papal legate to justify the restoration of the Patriarchate to the Greeks.[1]

Pope Paschal realized that he had made a mistake. Before long he was in correspondence with Alexius; and Alexius affected to overlook the whole episode. But it was not forgotten at Byzantium, and it increased the dislike of the average Byzantine against Rome.[2]

Over half a century passed before a Greek Patriarch was reintroduced into Antioch. When the Emperor John visited the city as its overlord in 1138, he found it more prudent not to insist on the installation of a Greek hierarchy. Pope Innocent II had just written to Antioch to forbid any Latin to remain in John's army should he take any steps against the Latin patriarchate; and John wanted to make a military alliance with the Latins.[3] But he found them so frivolous and unhelpful that four years later he marched again on Antioch, demanding that the city be handed over to him and promising to compensate the prince with territory elsewhere. This would have involved the restoration of the Greek Patriarchate. The prince rejected the suggestion on the ground that the Pope would disapprove; and John was about to take military action against Antioch at the time of his accidental death, in March 1143.[4]

His son, the Emperor Manuel, entered Antioch as its overlord in 1159. Its prince, Reynald of Châtillon, had three years previously indulged in a peculiarly savage and bloodthirsty raid against the Orthodox Imperial island of Cyprus, an action which had not endeared the Latins to

[1] Anna Comnena, op. cit. xii. 4, 8, xiii. 2–12, vol. iii, pp. 64–65, 77–85, 91–139.

[2] St. Cyril of Thrace, whose parents had made the pilgrimage to Rome and must therefore have had some Latin sympathies, showed himself violently hostile to Bohemond, whose defeat he foretold to the Emperor. Loparev, *Description of Various Lives of Greek Saints* (in Russian), pp. 381, 387.

[3] Runciman, op. cit. ii, pp. 211–19. Innocent II's letter is given in Rozière, *Cartulaire du Saint-Sépulcre*, p. 86.

[4] Runciman, op. cit. ii, pp. 222–4.

their Greek neighbours; and Manuel did everything possible to humiliate Reynald. Probably because Reynald was himself on very bad terms with the Latin Patriarch Aimery, Manuel did not intervene in ecclesiastical affairs.[1] But in 1165, when Reynald was a captive in Arab hands and the Prince of Antioch was Bohemond III, whose sister the Emperor had married, Manuel obliged Bohemond, in return for financial subsidies, to enthrone a Greek Patriarch, Athanasius II, and to fill vacant bishoprics with Greeks. The Latin, Aimery, retired protesting to a nearby castle; and his complaints were echoed in angry letters from Rome, threatening the Emperor and the prince with excommunication. But this episode was ended by an act of God. A great earthquake shook the city in 1170, and the roof of the cathedral came crashing down during divine service, burying the Greek Patriarch and many of his clergy in the ruins. The prince hastily restored Aimery to the patriarchal throne. The Emperor was not in a position at the moment to make an active protest.[2]

A Greek Patriarch was restored in Antioch in 1206 by Prince Bohemond IV. By this time Byzantium had been ruined by the Fourth Crusade. The prince had no fear that the Emperor would dominate him. On the contrary, he was frightened of the Armenians of Cilicia and annoyed with the Papacy for supporting them. The goodwill of his Greek subjects was useful to him. When the Pope excommunicated him and put the whole city under an interdict, he and the Latin laity in Antioch went happily to worship in Greek churches.[3] Once again the Latin line was soon restored;

[1] Runciman, op. cit. ii, pp. 351–4. [2] Ibid. pp. 371, 389.

[3] Cahen, *La Syrie du Nord au temps des Croisades*, pp. 612–13; Runciman, op. cit. iii, pp. 136–7. Symeon II's name does not appear on the lists of Antiochene Patriarchs kept at Constantinople. As the Byzantine world was in chaos as a result of the Fourth Crusade and the Emperor of Nicaea had not yet emerged as its leader, it would have been impossible for the Emperor to nominate him or for the Patriarch of Constantinople to ordain him. From the swift sequence of events it seems that he was already living in Antioch.

and, though the Mongols later insisted on the reintroduction of the Greeks,[1] it was not till the destruction of the Frankish Principality that the Greek line finally triumphed. But by that time Antioch lay in ruins and the Christian congregations were tragically reduced.[2]

We can definitely say that there was schism in the Church of Antioch from the year 1100 onwards. Though Greek clergy and congregations might be obliged to submit to a Latin hierarchy and, at times, Latin clergy and congregations to a Greek hierarchy, such submission was due only to governmental pressure. Each community owed sincere allegiance to its own Patriarch alone. But the cleavage was not absolute. There was intermarriage between the two communities, especially amongst the *bourgeois*. Even the Emperor Manuel had a Latin wife from Antioch, and Prince Bohemond III a Greek wife from Constantinople. It might have been happier for their relations had the Greeks and Latins admitted that they belonged to separate communities. As it was, each Patriarch claimed to represent the legitimate apostolic line from John the Oxite, and each community hoped to force its ritual and its hierarchy on the other. When in the thirteenth century the Papacy attempted to solve the problem by allowing the Greeks to keep their Patriarch and hierarchy so long as the supremacy of Rome was recognized, that is to say, by establishing the Greeks as a Uniate Church, it was too late. There had been too much bitterness already; and the compromise did not answer the question of the apostolic succession.[3]

[1] Bar-Hebraeus, *Chronography*, trans. Budge, p. 436; 'Lettre des Chrétiens de Terre Sainte à Charles d'Anjou', ed. Delaborde, *Revue de l'Orient latin*, vol. ii (1894), pp. 213–14. See Runciman, op. cit. iii, pp. 306–7, 319–20.

[2] The various Christian ecclesiastical organizations seem to have moved their headquarters from Antioch before the fifteenth century. When Bertrandon de la Broquière visited Antioch in 1432 he found only some 300 inhabited houses there and an almost entirely Moslem Turcoman population. De la Broquière, *Voyage d'Outremer*, ed. Schefer, pp. 84–85.

[3] Cahen, op. cit., pp. 684–5; Runciman, op. cit. iii, p. 231.

In the Patriarchate of Jerusalem the situation was different. The exiled Greek line of Patriarchs was unrecognized and almost unknown within the Patriarchate. There was no conscious breach there and not much dislike between the communities till Saladin reconquered Jerusalem itself for Islam. Hardly had he captured the city before an embassy arrived from Constantinople asking that the Patriarchate should be restored to the Greek candidate. The request seemed to the Latins to be yet another proof of Byzantine disloyalty to the cause, but it was not unreasonable. The Moslems certainly would not allow the native Christians in their new dominions to obey a Latin Patriarch living in the remnant of a kingdom that they were determined to destroy. The Greek Patriarch came from Constantinople and settled in the Holy City.[1] But Saladin refused a further request that the Holy Places should be put under the exclusive control of the Greeks. By his treaty with Cœur-de-Lion he allowed the Latins to retain establishments there, even in the Holy Sepulchre itself.[2] There were therefore from about 1188 onwards two lines of Patriarchs of Jerusalem living in the Holy Land, the Greek at Jerusalem and the Latin at Acre, each claiming to be in the apostolic succession. Meanwhile in the remaining Latin lands, as we can see from the *Assises des Bourgeois*, published at Acre in 1240, the Greeks, that is to say, the local Orthodox, were treated as a separate community.[3] This apparently had not been the case during the twelfth century. From 1229 to

[1] Dölger, *Regesten*, Nos. 1584, 1591, 1593, ii, pp. 94–95. Beha ed-Din, (Ibn Sheddad), *Life of Saladin*, trans. Conder (Palestine Pilgrims' Texts Society), pp. 198–201, tells of negotiations between Saladin and the Emperor.

[2] *Itinerarium Regis Ricardi*, ed. Stubbs, pp. 431–8; Ambroise, *L'Estoire de la Guerre Sainte*, ed. Paris, coll. 317–27; Beha ed-Din, op. cit., pp. 334–5.

[3] *Assises des Bourgeois*, *R.H.C. Lois*, vol. ii, pp. 178–9. For the date see Prawer, 'L'Etablissement des Coutumes de marché à Saint-Jean d'Acre', *Revue historique de Droit français et etranger*, Série 4, vol. xxix (1950), pp. 329 ff.

1244, when Jerusalem was once more in the Crusaders' hands, the Latin Patriarchs returned to the city, though they never took up permanent residence there. What happened to the Greek Patriarch during those years is a matter for conjecture.

The history of the Patriarchate of Alexandria is extremely obscure. The Patriarch Sophronius visited Constantinople in 1161; and the Patriarchs seem to have kept in touch with Constantinople, where most of their names were recorded on the diptychs.[1] For political reasons, as the subjects of a Moslem prince, they can have had little to do with the Franks in Palestine. But they freely gave communion to Latin merchants settled in Egypt and to Latin prisoners detained there; and they allowed the Latin chaplains to follow their own ritual. In about 1190 the Patriarch Mark of Alexandria wrote to the Byzantine canonist, Theodore Balsamon, to ask whether he should continue to communicate with Latins. Balsamon's uncompromisingly negative answer, which was followed by strictures on the Alexandrian Church for permitting practices of Coptic origin, seems to have annoyed Mark, who may have thought that Constantinople aimed to become as dictatorial as Rome.[2] Certainly his Patriarchate did not break off relations with the Papacy. The Patriarch Nicholas in the early thirteenth century not only ordained a Latin priest but also sent a representative to the Lateran Council of 1215.[3] But some time during the century relations were broken, perhaps under pressure from the Mameluk government, which did not carry on the sympathetic interest that many of the Ayubite princes had shown in Western affairs.

[1] See above, p. 69, n. 1. There is little direct evidence about the Alexandrian Patriarchate in the twelfth century.

[2] See below, p. 139.

[3] Innocent III was in communication with Nicholas of Alexandria, Potthast, *Regesta Pontificum Romanorum*, Nos. 1430, 4365, 4726, i, pp. 128, 376–7, 472–6. For the Alexandrian representative at the Lateran Council, see Hefele–Leclercq, *Histoire des Conciles*, v. 2, p. 1318.

In 1310 the Pope appointed a Latin Patriarch of Alexandria. Though the appointment was purely titular, it showed that Rome no longer recognized the Greek line.[1]

The fundamental cause of the schism between the three Eastern Patriarchates and Rome was, thus, the establishment of Crusader colonies in the Patriarchs' territories. The Patriarchs were at this period Greeks or the products of Greek schools. Their chief churches used the Byzantine liturgy, though the village churches kept to the vernacular. But they were not always well disposed to their brother of Constantinople and were always resentful if he made any attempt to dominate them. If they had to recognize an ecclesiastical superior, they would have preferred the distant domination of Rome. But during the centuries of Moslem rule they had looked to the Byzantine Emperor for protection against their secular masters; and the Patriarch of Antioch had been for more than a century under the direct lay authority of the Emperor. As Byzantine power faded, they might have welcomed a protector from farther to the West. But what they could not endure was to be ousted from their sees by Latin intruders who claimed to represent the legitimate line. Had the Papacy evolved the idea of Uniate Churches a century earlier and had it been prepared to admit that the native hierarchs were the lawful possessors of their sees while providing a Latin hierarchy for the colonists, it is possible that the Eastern Patriarchs would have accepted the supremacy of Rome without demur. In 1215 the Patriarch of Alexandria, where there was no Crusader hierarchy, seems to have acknowledged the authority of Innocent III at the Lateran Council. But it was too much to expect of the Crusaders that they should label themselves as intruders, conscious as they were of

[1] Le Quien, *Oriens Christianus*, iii, pp. 1141–4. A Latin bishop of Damietta was appointed in 1221 (*Chronica de Mailros*, ed. Bannatyne Club, Edinburgh, p. 138, stating that his salary was to be 1,000 talents). It is uncertain whether he was considered to be under the Patriarch of Alexandria or the Latin Patriarch of Jerusalem.

being the soldiers of the Pope. The Eastern Churches felt that they were being robbed of their legitimate and traditional rights by order of the Pope, who was moreover showing hostility to their natural protector, the Emperor at Constantinople. If they broke with Rome it was not because they wished to follow the lead of Constantinople but because the Pope trampled on their rights and also broke with the Emperor. Urban II's action in launching the Crusade in the East in pious hope that it would rescue the Eastern Churches and would please the Eastern Emperor produced results as far removed as possible from the intentions of the great Pope. The Crusaders brought not peace but a sword; and the sword was to sever Christendom.

V
DIPLOMACY AND DEBATE

THE difficulties that arose between the Oriental Patriarchates and Rome were mainly due to the intrusion and colonization of the Crusaders in Eastern lands. The controversy between Constantinople and Rome in the twelfth century was subtler and more complicated in origin. Rome never quite understood the situation at Constantinople. The Pope saw that the Emperor dictated to the Church and was inclined to assume that the Church would therefore obey any Imperial order. But in fact the Emperor's Caesaropapism was not unlimited. No Emperor could afford to go against public opinion. He could not flout the accepted laws and traditions of the Empire. Not only was there a powerful and well-educated lay society within the Empire, but the people of Constantinople held strong views and prejudices and never failed to express them, and in moulding these views the clergy was more influential than the Imperial Court. Even Alexius Comnenus, whose attempts to reform the Byzantine Church were guided by patriotic necessity, won from them long periods of unpopularity and was rewarded by conspiracies against his person. Experience soon taught him the limits up to which he could go.

Alexius himself, his son John, and his grandson Manuel were all of them anxious to keep on good terms with Rome, partly from a sincere desire to preserve peace in Christendom and partly from a careful appreciation of the diplomatic value of Roman friendship. Throughout the greater part of the twelfth century the policy of the Imperial Court was to avoid any breach with the Western Church. But the Byzantine clergy was not impressed by the Emperor's political calculations. The Church of Constantinople was conscious of being the Church of the greatest city in Christendom. During the last centuries it had come to despise the Church of Rome, not without reason. The strength of the sudden revival of the Papacy was misunderstood at Constantinople; and the papal claims for world dominion seemed ludicrously arrogant. Byzantine ecclesiastical pride was enhanced by a genuine disapproval of certain Western practices such as the use of unleavened bread and by a resentful horror that Rome should apparently insist on a unilateral alteration in the accepted Creed of Christendom. Any move that implied a surrender to Rome would therefore be met with the passionate opposition of the Byzantine Church. Lay public opinion at Constantinople was at first less heated. When the Crusades began the people of the Empire were ready to welcome the Westerners as fellow Christians. But the unruliness and unfriendliness of the Western soldiers soon provoked dislike; while the increasing numbers of Italian merchants who settled within the Empire and began to capture all its commerce added to the resentment of the Byzantines against the Latins. The ground was thus well prepared for the propaganda against the West that the Church began to spread. The Emperor for all his power was obliged to tread warily. Yet even the clergy were not yet ready to face up to the idea of schism. Everyone clung as long as possible to the belief that the Christian Church was still one and undivided.

The Latin chroniclers of the First Crusade expressed this belief. They regarded Constantinople as a particularly holy city. Robert the Monk declared that you could call it the equal of Rome in holiness and majesty, were it not that Rome was the seat of the Papacy. Guibert of Nogent proclaimed that it was worthy of the respect of the whole world, and Ekkehard of Aura that it deserved its divine protection.[1] Throughout the First Crusade there was

[1] Robert the Monk, *Historia Hierosolymitana*, *R.H.C.Occ.*, vol. iii, p. 750; Guibert of Nogent, *Historia Hierosolymitana*, *R.H.C.Occ.*, vol. iv, p. 132; Ekkehard of Aura, *Hierosolymita*, ed. Hagenmeyer, pp. 69–70.

mutual goodwill on the popular level. Badly though Peter the Hermit's followers behaved they were pleased with the welcome given them by the Balkan populace, by whom Peter himself was regarded with respect.[1] There was a curious episode at Athens in 1099 when some Crusaders on their way by sea to Palestine were forced by the weather to land at Piraeus. The Governor of Athens was suspicious of them, thinking them to be pirates; but they appealed to a local hermit, Meletius, who welcomed them as his brothers and persuaded the authorities and the people of Athens to treat them kindly.[2]

This goodwill was thrown away chiefly by the lawlessness of the Crusaders. The suspicions of the Athenian governor are understandable when we remember that a few months previously a Pisan squadron conveying the Archbishop of Pisa, who had some sort of legatine power from the Pope, had paused to raid Corfu, Lefcas, and Zante.[3] Even the tolerant Theophylact of Bulgaria, through whose diocese many Crusading armies passed, compared the experience to a barbarian invasion, though he said that he and his flock were ready to bear the inconvenience with patience. At Constantinople the populace was horrified by the thieving and destructive habits of the Crusader soldiers, who soon sensed and reciprocated the dislike that they aroused. But on each side blame was thrown on the authorities of the other side. When things went wrong the average Crusader blamed not the Byzantine people but the Emperor and his advisers. He despised the Greeks—'the

[1] Anna Comnena speaks in kindly terms of Peter. See below, p. 111. The friendliness of the peasants in the Balkans, when they were not being actually robbed, is reported by Albert of Aix, *Liber Christianae Expeditionis*, i. 13–15, *R.H.C.Occ.*, vol. iv, pp. 282–3. It was a Greek whose courageous escape from Civetot brought rescue to the People's Army after the disaster there. Ibid. i. 22, p. 289.

[2] Nicholas of Methone, *Βίος Μελετίου τοῦ Νέου*, ed. Vasilievsky, *Publications of the Palestinian–Russian Society* (in Russian), vol. vi (1886), fasc. 17, p. 32, and introduction, pp. xxviii–xxxii.

[3] Anna Comnena, *Alexiad*, xi. 10, ed. Leib, iii, pp. 41–44.

wretched little Greeks, the most feeble of men', as Guibert of Nogent called them[1]—but it was as yet only their rulers against whom he felt resentment. The Byzantines for their part were prepared to regard the Crusader pilgrims and soldiers as fellow Christians, but allotted the responsibility for their riotousness and truculence on their leaders.

But amongst these leaders were the Latin bishops and clergy. The Byzantines were deeply shocked to see in the Crusader armies so many priests who bore arms and went into battle.[2] This outraged Eastern sentiment, which was horrified that men dedicated to God should take part in warfare. They listened therefore all the more willingly to the strictures of the Greek clergy against their Latin colleagues. It was moreover known in educated circles in Byzantium that the Pope claimed supreme authority in the West, and when the Western princes and clerics showed hostility the hostility was attributed to the Pope. Had not Gregory VII encouraged Guiscard against Byzantium, and Paschal II Bohemond? The friendliness of Urban II was ignored. Rome was felt to be behind the aggressive enmity of the Western princes.

The Emperor Alexius, who was well aware of the importance of the Pope's influence and the potential value of his friendship, had to act with circumspection. His main object was to reconquer land in Asia from the Turks. It was essential for him to have security on his western frontier, and, in particular, to end the danger of Norman aggression. About the time of his reconciliation with Urban II, Alexius entered into a private correspondence with the Abbot of Monte Cassino, Oderisius, one of the most respected and disinterested prelates in Italy. Cordial letters were exchanged, which made no mention of awkward subjects like the *Filioque* clause or the use of unleavened bread. The Emperor confided in the abbot about his anxiety to help the

[1] Guibert of Nogent, op. cit., p. 154.
[2] See above, p. 83, n. 2.

Crusaders and hinted that co-operation was not always easy.[1] When Oderisius died in 1105 his successors Otho and Girard carried on the correspondence, though it was probably interrupted when Paschal fell victim to Bohemond's blandishments. In spite of the interruption Alexius continued to show that he had no ill will towards the Latin Church. At some time about then he founded a hospice for Western pilgrims at Civetot and entrusted it to the Cluniacs.[2] When therefore in 1111 he let it be known that he was willing to draw closer to the Pope he had friends in Italy who were glad to act as intermediaries. The time seemed to him ripe for establishing firm alliances if not an actual outpost in Italy. The Norman dominions were under the rule of three inoffensive dowagers, Adela of Flanders at Naples, Constance of France at Taranto, and Adelaide of Montferrat at Palermo. The Emperor and the Pope could embark on a diplomatic offensive without Norman interference.

Pope Paschal was equally eager for a political understanding. The temporary weakness of the Normans had left him without a local lay protector against the Germans. In 1111 the German king Henry V had marched on Rome and imprisoned him, and had obliged him to crown him Emperor and to make concessions that the Pope promptly regretted. In January 1112 Alexius sent Girard of Monte Cassino a letter in which he mentioned his distress at hearing of the Pope's imprisonment.[3] He followed it with a

[1] Alexius Comnenus, letters, in Hagenmeyer, *Kreuzzugsbriefe*, pp. 140–1, 152–3. The monks of Monte Cassino considered Alexius as a particularly devoted friend and patron. Peter Diaconus, *Chronica Monasterii Casinensis*, *M.G.H.Ss.*, vol. vii, pp. 770, 792.

[2] See below, p. 114. The date when Alexius endowed the Cluniac establishment at Civetot is unknown. Anna Comnena, op. cit. x. 6, vol. ii, pp. 211–12, talks of the Latins having erected fortified buildings on the site of the battle of Civetot and having used the bones of the victims as mortar. The Cluniac hospice was presumably connected with this macabre construction.

[3] Riant, *Inventaire critique des lettres historiques des Croisades*, pp. 138–40.

letter to the authorities of the city of Rome, congratulating them on their courageous support of the Pope and apparently suggesting to them that he was willing to accept the Imperial crown of the West for himself or for his son John. The Romans responded by sending an encouraging embassy to Constantinople; and Alexius promised the envoys that he would come to Rome himself that summer. When the summer arrived he was unwell and could not make the journey. Indeed, we may doubt if he ever took the scheme seriously; but it served to give him influence in Italy. Instead of making the journey himself he sent a personal ambassador to the Pope.[1]

Had Paschal considered Alexius to be a schismatic prince he would never have allowed the negotiations to go so far. But he was anxious to clear up the ecclesiastical situation before he would take further political steps. At the end of 1112 he wrote a letter to Alexius in which he asked that the relations between the Churches should first be put on a proper basis. He reminded the Emperor how subservient the Patriarch of Constantinople used to be to Rome in the old days, whereas now the Patriarch refused to receive his letters or his legates. He complained, a little querulously, that he had a harder task than the Emperor because he had to govern so many diverse peoples whereas the Emperor was master of his Empire and his clergy. The first thing, Paschal maintained, was that his 'confrater' of Constantinople should recognize the primacy and dignity of the Roman See. When that was done, a general council could be held and the points at issue discussed and resolved.[2]

Paschal's letter was honest and logical. He proposed a return to the situation in the sixth and seventh centuries, when the Emperor could browbeat the Patriarch into showing a due deference to Rome. But things had altered since

[1] Peter Diaconus, op. cit., p. 785; Chalandon, *Essai sur le règne d'Alexis Ier Comnène*, p. 261.

[2] Paschal II, *Epistolae*, *M.P.L.*, vol. clxiii, coll. 388–90.

then, and Byzantine public opinion had hardened. For all his power over the Church the Emperor could not now make the Patriarch obey such instructions. It is unlikely that he even tried to do so. The papal legates who brought the letter seem to have been put off with an equivocal answer.[1]

A year later, at the end of 1113 or early in 1114, Peter Chrysolan (or Grosolano), Archbishop of Milan, came to Constantinople and was invited to discuss with Greek theologians in the presence of the Emperor the question of the Holy Ghost and the azymes.[2] Amongst the unhappy delusions of mankind is the belief that a dispute can be settled by a debate. The contrary is true; for neither side will admit defeat but instead will assemble more and more arguments to confound its opponents. Paschal's letter might have been kept secret by the Emperor; but the debate with Chrysolan produced the very effect that Alexius must most have dreaded. It let loose a torrent of polemical arguments from the Greek ecclesiastics. During the last few years there had been a lull in the controversy. The only anti-Latin work to be produced had been a treatise against the azymites written by John the Oxite, ex-Patriarch of Antioch. It is a work that gives the usual symbolic arguments and quotations from the Fathers; but John's personal experiences gave a certain bitterness to his tone, careful though he is to recommend the virtues of moderation.[3] Now a number of writers took up their pens to answer Chrysolan. The official exponents of the Greek Church's view were Eustratius, Metropolitan of Nicaea, and the Abbot John Phurnes, who published the arguments that they had used in the debate.[4] They were

[1] Chalandon, op. cit., p. 262.

[2] Ibid., p. 263. Chrysolan's oration is given in full in *M.P.G.*, vol. cxxvii, coll. 911–20.

[3] John's treatise, which may have been written as part of the polemic against Chrysolan, is published by Leib, 'Deux Inédits Byzantines sur les Azymites', *Orientalia Christiana*, vol. ii (1924), pp. 244–63.

[4] Eustratius's orations are published in Demetracopoulos, *Bibliothèque ecclésiastique*, i, pp. 47–198, and John Phurnes's, ibid., pp. 36 ff. See

supported by treatises written by two other ecclesiastics, Nicetas Seides of Iconium and the historian monk, John Zonaras, and by two laymen, the poet Theodore Prodromus and the philosopher Theodore of Smyrna. The publicity given to the debate had clearly aroused passionate interest.[1]

The debates were inevitably inconclusive. Both Chrysolan and his opponents were accomplished controversialists, whose arguments were logical and well founded. But the reader who goes through the long reports and treatises soon realizes that in fact neither side answers the other; for their arguments are built upon different premisses. The Latin argument on the *Filioque* seems at first sight to be clearer and more convincing than the Greek; but the Latin conception of the Trinity is less subtle and delicately balanced, and Chrysolan's careful arguments are irrelevant to his opponents' fundamental attitude. On the question of the azymes the Greeks have a more impressive list of patristic texts to support their point of view; but the Latins were unlikely to regard a few citations from the Fathers as providing an unanswerable argument. The only solution would have been for each Church to show the Economy so often recommended by Orthodox theologians. But Rome was not in the mood to allow divergences, while the Greeks, though they might be willing to show tolerance over purely theological points and practices, could not bring themselves to forgive an addition to the Creed which they considered a direct challenge to the authority of the Oecumenical Councils. Nor were they prepared to admit that any of their old-established usages could be wrong. The essential issue was the question of papal authority. Could the Pope add to the Creed at his pleasure, and could he even insist on uniformity of usage? But, owing probably to the express wishes of

Krumbacher, *Geschichte der byzantinischen Litteratur*, p. 85, and Demetracopoulos, *Graecia Orthodoxa*, pp. 11–12.

[1] Krumbacher, op. cit., pp. 85–87; Demetracopoulos, *Graecia Orthodoxa*, pp. 12–21.

the Emperor, the question of papal authority was not raised during the debate.

Alexius was certainly eager to avoid discussions that might go too far. When his favourite theologian, Euthymius Zigabenus, published his *Panoplia Dogmatica*, which was intended as an official statement on heresies, the question of unleavened bread is relegated to the chapter on Armenian malpractices. Not a word is said against the Latins there. Though the question of the Holy Ghost is treated at some length, the only section that deals with the *Filioque* is a transcription of the treatise that Photius had written on the subject, which appears to have been added by some pious scribe to Zigabenus's original work.[1] But the Emperor seems to have felt some resentment against two individual Popes, Gregory VII and Paschal II, both of whom had treated him badly; and this resentment is echoed in the pages of the biography written about him by his daughter Anna Comnena.

Anna wrote her great work some time after the year 1140. She had by then been living some twenty years in retirement. Since her father's death in 1118 she had no further access to official documents; and her opinions had been modified by her long absence from the Court and affected by the monastic circles in which she now moved.[2] She assumes throughout her work that the Greeks and Latins are in full communion with each other. She believes that ordinations were and should be interchangeable between the two Churches. In the Treaty of Devol, when Alexius insisted that a Greek should be restored to the patriarchal

[1] The *Panoplia* is published in *M.P.G.*, vol. cxxx. The earliest extant manuscript contains the chapter taken from Photius, but it is not contemporary with the author. It is difficult to believe that Zigabenus, who was a profound and eager theologian, would not have written his own argument on the matter if he had wished to raise it at all. It is significant that he says nothing about the Latins when dealing with azymes.

[2] See Buckler, *Anna Comnena*, *passim*, esp. Books II and V, for a general analysis of Anna's circumstances and views.

throne of Antioch, it was added that as a matter of course the Greek Patriarch should perform all ordinations, for the Latin clergy as well as for the Greek.[1] Much as Anna deplored the barbarism of the Crusaders and the arrogance and perfidy of their leaders, she considered that they were the soldiers of Christ and could count on the goodwill of God.[2] She was sympathetic with the aims of the simpler pilgrims, who, she said, 'truly wished to worship at the Lord's tomb and to see for themselves the Holy Places'.[3] She gives Latin bishops the title of 'most beloved of God'.[4] But as soon as she starts to talk about the Papacy her tone changes. She mentions no Pope by name. The whole reign of Urban II, with whom her father was on excellent terms, is passed over in silence. She does not allow him any part in the launching of the Crusade. One almost has the impression that she could not bear to speak well of any Pope but was too scrupulous to speak ill of Urban. Though Gregory VII is not mentioned by name she gives a full and extremely inaccurate account of his quarrel with Henry IV over investitures. According to her the German king accused the Pope of usurpation because he had seized the apostolic throne without the king's consent, while the Pope on his side accused the king of selling benefices to unworthy men for money or for gifts. When the king sent a threatening embassy to the Pope, the latter imprisoned and mutilated the ambassadors; and Anna describes their experiences with relish, hinting that there were further outrages which would be unsuitable for a woman and a princess to mention.[5] In fact Gregory protected the ambassadors from an ugly demonstration by the Roman crowd; but Anna

[1] Anna Comnena, op. cit. xiii. 12, vol. iii, p. 134.

[2] Anna's account of the discovery of the Holy Lance at Antioch shows a genuine respect for the piety of the Crusaders. Op. cit. xi. 6, vol. iii, pp. 30–31.

[3] Ibid. x. 5, vol. ii, p. 209.

[4] *Θεοφιλέστατος*. No Latin bishop is mentioned without this epithet.

[5] Ibid. i. 12, vol. i, pp. 47–49.

chose to believe a rumour put about by the Pope's enemies in Germany.[1] She speaks with disapproval of the Pope's declaration of war against the German king and with contempt of his need to secure the help of the Normans.[2] But she never mentions Gregory's excommunication of her father, nor does she suggest that the Normans were influenced by this excommunication in their first attack on the Empire, nor yet that the Pope was influenced by Guiscard's production of an impostor to impersonate the fallen Emperor Michael. For some reason she minimizes the Pope's part in encouraging Guiscard against Byzantium. It is only when she reaches Bohemond's later career and events that occurred within her own adult memory that she accuses the Papacy of abetting the Normans. She tells how Bohemond tricked the Pope—Paschal II—into supporting him by showing him some of the Emperor's Petcheneg auxiliaries whom he had captured and declaring that Alexius was employing these heathen barbarians to fight against the Christian Crusaders. That is to say, it was only from foolish ignorance that Paschal gave his backing to Bohemond. But she makes it clear how bitterly his action was resented in Byzantium.[3] About the papal claims she held strong and inaccurate views. Talking of Gregory's supposed outrage on the German ambassadors she says:

This was the deed of a Pontiff, yes, of the Supreme Pontiff, the deed of the man who claims to preside over the whole world, or so the Latins say and believe, so great is their arrogance. But really, when the seat of Empire was transferred from over there to our country and our Imperial city, together with the Senate and all the administration, the chief rank in the episcopal hierarchy was transferred at the same time. Ever since that time the Emperors have given precedence to the See of Constantinople; and, above all, the Council of Chalcedon raised the Bishop of Constantinople to the

[1] See Buckler, op. cit., p. 308.
[2] Anna Comnena, op. cit., loc. cit.
[3] Ibid. xii. 8, vol. iii, pp. 79–80.

highest place and subordinated to it all the bishoprics in the Oecumene.[1]

Even if Anna employed the word 'Oecumene' in its usual Byzantine sense to mean the Empire, her statement is untrue. Thessalonica, for instance, remained subordinate to Rome till the eighth century. And her interpretation of the 28th Canon of Chalcedon is demonstrably incorrect. Anna was on the whole a careful writer, conscientious about her sources, and proud of her theological learning. But here she seems to have been so sure of herself that she did not trouble to verify her statements. If she with all her education believed that the primacy itself had been transferred to Constantinople at Chalcedon, it must have been the belief of large sections of the Byzantine world, to whom therefore the claims of the Roman See would seem outrageously pretentious and wrong. To accept them would be to deprive Constantinople of her position as capital of the Christian world. National pride would never permit such an abdication.

It should be added that the official Eastern Church has never given such an interpretation to the 28th Canon of Chalcedon. Its view is that Rome indeed enjoyed the honorary primacy till she forfeited it by exaggerating her claims and by tampering with the Creed. But as yet the official view was not specifically formulated.

Alexius I's successor, John II, carried on his father's Western policy. He wished to retain allies in Italy, particularly for use against the Normans. He was ready to enter into friendly negotiations with either the Pope or the Western Emperor as it might suit him. He freely planned matrimonial alliances between members of his own house and Western royal families. But, though his letters to the Pope were full of pious sentiments about the need for a closer understanding between the two Churches, he was careful

[1] Ibid. i. 12, vol. i, p. 48.

never to commit himself or his clergy too far. During the early years of his reign there was an atmosphere of cordiality. About the year 1120 we find Peter the Venerable, the last great Abbot of Cluny, writing to the Emperor who, he says, has been appointed to watch over all the Churches of the world, to ask him to continue to show his Imperial favour to the Cluniac house at Civetot which his father had founded and endowed.[1] At the same time Peter wrote to the Patriarch of Constantinople, addressing him as 'the venerable and great Pontiff of God at Constantinople'. In a letter of remarkable friendliness he talks of his desire to visit the Imperial capital, 'the Christian city founded by Jesus Christ and the Emperor Constantine', and to see its churches and relics.

> I should then [he says] see your face, which I long to contemplate; I should venerate in you all the blessed pontiffs of your city. . . . We would conclude an indissoluble pact together and swear to our mutual spiritual love, if you would agree. I would beg of you by word of mouth what I now ask from far off, that you and your people would of your charity give us, myself and the flock of Cluny, your prayers and those of your people; and we should give you ours with equal affection.[2]

After reading this letter one can only comment that if the Churches had been in schism since 1054 Abbot Peter was unaware of it.

Diplomatic exchanges went on, but they produced no concrete results. Nothing came of the embassy sent by the Emperor John to Pope Calixtus II in 1124, nor of the return embassy sent by Pope Honorius II to the Emperor two years later.[3] Theological debates seem to have been avoided, fortunately, for they only served to emphasize differences. In 1136 the Western Emperor Lothair III's ambassador,

[1] Peter the Venerable, letter No. 39, *M.P.L.*, vol. clxxxix, coll. 260–1.
[2] Peter the Venerable, letter No. 41, ibid., coll. 261–2.
[3] Theiner, *Monumenta Spectantia ad Unionem Ecclesiarum Graecae et Romanae*, pp. 1–4.

Bishop Anselm of Havelberg, visited Constantinople in order to discuss the possibility of common action by the two empires against Roger II of Sicily. Anselm was well received, and politically his mission was successful. During its course he was offered an opportunity to take part in a debate in the presence of the Emperor on the theological points of difference between the Churches. His opponent was Nicetas, Archbishop of Nicomedia. To judge from the report that Anselm forwarded some years later to Pope Eugenius III, the disputants were courteous and good-tempered and the official interpreter, the Italian Moses of Bergamo, performed his task with conscientious correctitude. Indeed, so clearly does Anselm report the Byzantine case against the papal claims that, loyal though he was to his Church, he gives the impression of having enjoyed as a German bishop showing the Italian Pope and the Roman Court that there was another side to the question.[1]

The two chief subjects of the debate were the Procession of the Holy Ghost and the use of unleavened bread. With regard to the former Archbishop Nicetas declared that he was prepared to agree that the Holy Ghost proceeded through the Son but not from the Son. He hoped that that formula, which most of the subsequent Greek theologians have been willing to permit, would satisfy the desire of the Latins for elucidation, though he did not consider that even those words should actually be added to the Creed.[2] With regard to unleavened bread, he showed that the views expressed by different Popes were contradictory. He quoted from the fourth-century Popes Melchiades and Siricius words that indicated clearly that they assumed the bread used at the Sacrament to be leavened. 'If', he says, 'the authority of the Roman Pontiffs seems to be sufficient for you to use against me it should equally suffice for me to use

[1] Anselm's report is given in d'Achery, *Spicilegium sive Collectio veterum aliquot Scriptorum* (1723 edition), i, pp. 161 ff.

[2] Ibid., p. 190.

against you.'[1] But Nicetas soon emphasized that he did not himself consider papal authority to provide an unanswerable argument. The essence of his views is given in the following speech.

> My dearest brother, we do not deny to the Roman Church the primacy amongst the five sister Patriarchates; and we recognize her right to the most honourable seat at an Oecumenical Council. But she has separated herself from us by her own deeds when through pride she assumed a monarchy which does not belong to her office. . . . How shall we accept from her decrees that have been issued without consulting us and even without our knowledge? If the Roman Pontiff, seated on the lofty throne of his glory, wishes to thunder at us and, so to speak, hurl his mandates at us from on high, and if he wishes to judge us and even to rule us and our Churches, not by taking counsel with us but at his own arbitrary pleasure, what kind of brotherhood, or even what kind of parenthood can this be? We should be the slaves, not the sons, of such a Church, and the Roman See would be not the pious mother of sons but a hard and imperious mistress of slaves.

'What', cries Nicetas, with all the pride of Byzantine culture behind him, 'would be the use of all our Greek learning, of all our knowledge of the Scriptures and the Fathers?' Nicetas concludes this speech by recommending the Papacy to be more humble if it wishes to find fellow workers in the vineyard of Christ. 'I ask your pardon,' he adds, 'when I say this about the Roman Church, for I venerate her along with you. But I cannot follow her along with you through everything; nor do I think that she should necessarily be followed through everything.'[2]

Anselm answered that Rome deserved to be supreme judge because her judgements had always been correct. She had never lapsed into heresy. He then put forward the traditional argument of the Petrine claims.[3] But Nicetas

[1] d'Achery, op. cit., p. 200. Pope Melchiades does indeed speak of the Bread as 'fermentum' (*Liber Pontificalis*, ed. Duchesne, i, pp. 74–75).

[2] d'Achery, op. cit., p. 196.

[3] Ibid., p. 197.

would have none of it. He replied that the Holy Spirit did not descend to Saint Peter alone at Pentecost. All the Apostles, he said, were given the power to bind and to loose; and he considered that all Christians had the right to be consulted on matters of discipline and doctrine. The actual doctrinal and ritual issues did not seem to him to be insoluble. An Oecumenical Council could, he thought, settle them. But he refused to submit to dictation from Rome; for, to quote him again, 'the Roman Pontiff is not the Prince of Priests nor the supreme priest nor anything of the sort, but merely the bishop of the leading See'.[1]

Nicetas, like Theophylact of Bulgaria half a century earlier, belonged to the liberal wing of the Byzantine Church. He did not wish to break the unity of Christendom on a ritual or even a doctrinal difference; but he would not allow that the Pope could add to the Creed of the Councils and he was firmly opposed to any subjection of the Byzantine ecclesiastical organization to Rome. There were a few ecclesiastics who were willing to go further in friendliness to Rome. Nicetas of Maronea, Chartophylax at Constantinople and later Archbishop of Thessalonica, saw no doctrinal objection to the *Filioque* clause and could not see why his compatriots were only prepared to allow *per Filium*, which, he thought, came to the same thing. But he thought that Rome was wrong to insist on its addition to the Creed. As regards the schism, he blamed his own Church for starting it and deplored the Byzantine attitude of hostility to Rome. But he would not commit himself to recognize the full papal claims.[2] The Armenian philosopher Theorianus, who made it his task to try to reconcile his native Church with the Byzantine, told both the Armenians and the Byzantines that they should not separate themselves from the Orthodox See of Rome. But he too was silent over

[1] Ibid.

[2] Nicetas Chartophylax, *Dialogi de Spiritu Sancto*, *M.P.G.*, vol. cxxxix, coll. 224 ff.

the question of authority.[1] Such views, however, were rare. Most Byzantine churchmen were openly hostile to Rome; and the Byzantines in general were shocked by the Pope's intervention into secular politics. They had no love for the German king, to whom they would never concede the title of Emperor; but they were horrified at the Bishop of Rome actually declaring war on an anointed monarch. It was that aspect of Gregory VII's career that roused Anna Comnena's deepest disapproval. About the same time as Anselm's embassy to Constantinople a Byzantine ambassador, whose name is unrecorded but who was apparently a layman, called at the Abbey of Monte Cassino on his way to the Emperor Lothair's court. There he had an argument with Peter the Deacon, the official chronicler of the abbey. They discussed the Creed; and when the ambassador accused the Latins of unjustifiably adding the word *Filioque* after *Patre*, Peter smartly retorted that the Greeks, too, added to the Creed by insisting on putting the word *solo* there. Like most wisecracks it was unfair; the Greeks never proposed that *solo* should be officially added. But the Latins genuinely believed that by insisting on Procession from the Father alone the Greeks were damaging the indivisibility of the Trinity. It was not, however, the theological point that worried the ambassador most. 'Your Pope has become an Emperor', he complained; and he added that he could not approve of a Church 'whose bishops rush into wars, as your Pope Innocent is doing, distributing money, assembling soldiers and generally assuming the purple'.[2]

The Emperor Manuel, who succeeded to the throne in 1140, shared his father John's desire for a political understanding with Rome; and he had moreover a personal liking for Western folk and their ways. In spite of the deepening animosity between the Greek and Latin peoples, due in the

[1] Theorianus, letters, in *M.P.G.* vol. cxxxiii, col. 258. See Tournebize, *Histoire politique et religieuse de l'Arménie*, pp. 245–53.

[2] Peter Diaconus, op. cit., *M.G.H.Ss.*, vol. vii, p. 833.

main to the Crusades, he encouraged diplomatic exchanges and theological debates and went out of his way to show his own goodwill towards Rome and the West. In 1154 Bishop Anselm of Havelberg paid a second visit to Constantinople, and on his homeward journey he stopped at Thessalonica, where he had a debate with the Archbishop, Basil of Ochrida. The same ground was covered as by Anselm's debate with Nicetas, though Basil was not quite such a courteous controversialist. Once again the rights and wrongs of the *Filioque* clause and the use of unleavened bread were argued inconclusively; but once again papal supremacy proved to be the real stumbling-block.[1] During the following year Pope Hadrian IV wrote to Archbishop Basil to ask him to show kindness to two papal envoys who were on their way through Thessalonica to the Emperor's Court to negotiate a political alliance against the Normans. Unfortunately the letter of introduction contained a long restatement of papal claims. It referred to the members of the Greek Church as 'lost sheep', and it declared that the councils had ordained the reference of every ecclesiastical dispute to the judgement of Rome.[2] Basil wrote back a letter of almost exaggerated politeness, saying that the Pope would certainly be entitled to call the Greeks 'lost sheep' had they added to the Creed or adopted the use of unleavened bread. But, he remarked, the differences between the two Churches were really very small and could be resolved by goodwill between 'the Bishops who act under your direction and us who in the East accept the splendour of the priesthood of the sublime throne of Constantinople'. That is to say, he made it quite clear that he considered the two Churches to be equal in standing; and he added that it was for the Pope to show goodwill first.[3]

[1] Schmidt, *Des Basilius aus Achrida, Erzbischofs von Thessalonich, bisher unedierte Dialoge*, passim.

[2] Mansi, *Sacrorum Conciliorum Collectio*, vol. xxi, p. 795.

[3] Ibid., pp. 799–802.

It must have been obvious that these efforts for ecclesiastical reconciliation were doomed to fail, unless there were a fundamental change in the temper both of Rome and of Byzantium. But neither the Emperor nor the Pope wished for a breach. Manuel's occidental tastes and ambitions were encouraged by the periodical desire of the Papacy to find a lay protector against the aggression of the Normans or of the Western Emperor. Manuel continued to write letters proclaiming his eagerness to unite the Greek Church to the Mother-Church of Rome, 'as it had been in the old times', sheltering behind a phrase that was friendly but vague.[1] On his side Pope Alexander III began to question the whole conception of the Western Empire and to wonder whether it might not be wiser to recognize Manuel as the sole legitimate Emperor. It is doubtful whether he would have supported the Byzantine theory, which, according to the historian John Cinnamus, was that the Roman Emperor, that is to say, the Emperor at Constantinople, was the proper person to make appointments to the papal throne, but, as the Emperors had neglected this duty, Popes were suitably elected by the clergy of the see, and that the German king had no business to interfere.[2] Though the Pope as an ecclesiastic ought not himself to take up arms against a secular monarch, he was absolutely correct in applying to the legitimate Emperor to protect his rights, if necessary by war. Pope Alexander III would not have subscribed to all of this; but his attitude encouraged Manuel, who was incurably optimistic, to picture himself as ruling in Old Rome as well as in Constantinople. In 1166 the Emperor offered the union of the Churches in return for a coronation at Rome. In 1169 his plans seemed to be so near to realization that he wrote to Alexander to suggest that when his troops entered Rome he should unite the Churches of Rome

[1] Manuel Comnenus, letters cited in Watterich, *Pontificum Romanorum Vitae*, ii, pp. 404, 410.

[2] Cinnamus, *Epitome Historiarum* (Bonn edition), p. 229.

and Constantinople by the simple device of appointing the Pope to the Patriarchate. The Patriarch Luke Chrysoberges had died early that year; and it was doubtless the vacancy in the Patriarchate that gave Manuel this remarkable idea. The Pope was somewhat embarrassed. He replied promising to give the Emperor his support in all secular matters. He had already in the past offered him, in the words of a hostile German writer, 'every vanity of vanities, which Manuel himself did not expect'.[1] But he thought Manuel's present ecclesiastical solution unnecessary. It would be far better if the Patriarch would just agree to his three small requests: first, to recognize his primacy; secondly, to admit the right of appeal to Rome; and, thirdly, to commemorate him in the diptychs of Constantinople.[2] The Emperor might have been able to induce his Church to accede to two of the demands. If the Pope were to be mentioned in the diptychs, then his primacy, which had never been denied him by official opinion in the Eastern Churches, would automatically be restored to him. But even there difficulties arose. Byzantine procedure demanded that a Declaration of Faith should be sent before a pontiff's name could be inserted in the diptychs, and unless the Pope omitted the *Filioque* in his recital of the Creed his declaration would not be accepted. Moreover, to Byzantium primacy meant merely an honorary rank whereas to Rome it implied supremacy. But the right of appeal to Rome was something that the Church of Constantinople would never now admit.

Manuel had not been able to postpone the election of a new Patriarch, Michael of Anchialus; and when the Emperor sent the Pope's letter on to him Michael replied with a strongly worded memorandum in which he dealt almost

[1] Burchard in Sudendorf, *Registrum für die deutsche Geschichte*, ii, p. 138 (dated December 1161).

[2] *Liber Pontificalis*, ii, pp. 419–20 (Boso, *Vita Alexandri III*); Cinnamus, op. cit., p. 262; Allatius, *De Ecclesiae Occidentalis atque Orientalis perpetua Consensione*, ii, pp. 664–5; and below, following note.

exclusively with the Petrine claims of Rome. He would have none of them. If Rome had enjoyed the primacy, it was because of the dignity of the City of Rome, not because of any apostolic primacy. If Rome's claims were based on Saint Peter's tenure of the see, what, he asked, of Antioch, which was also the See of Saint Peter and had been founded before the See of Rome? What, indeed, of Jerusalem, where Christ Himself had taught and suffered? His view was that the government of the Universal Church should depend upon present-day considerations rather than on the inconclusive evidence of apostolic foundations. Constantinople had been chosen by God to be the seat of the Christian Empire. Whatever respect the older Patriarchates and particularly Rome might rightly command, he thought it ridiculous that the supreme ecclesiastical government of the Empire should reside in any city other than the Imperial capital. His repugnance against submission to an alien religious authority carried him further. He would sooner, he said, see his Church under the secular domination of the infidel than under the spiritual domination of the West. 'Let the Moslem be my material master', he declared, 'rather than the Latin my spiritual master. If I am subject to the former, at least he will not force me to share his faith. But if I have to be united in religion to the latter, under his control, I may have to separate myself from God.'[1]

This extremist view was to recur later in Byzantine history, attaining its best known expression on the eve of the Turkish conquest, when the Grand Duke Lucas Notaras announced that he preferred the sultan's turban to the cardinal's hat. At first sight it seems an example of narrow sectarianism; but it was based both on reason and on instinct. The Byzantines genuinely feared that they would be untrue to the great traditions of their past and the high

[1] Michael of Anchialus, *Dialogue*, given in Loparev, 'On the Unionism of the Emperor Manuel Comnenus' (in Russian), *Vizantiiskii Vremennik*, vol. xiv (1917), pp. 344–57.

standards of their present if they let themselves be absorbed into the West, which they regarded, with some justification, as barbarous, crude, and ungodly. Michael's attitude was not helpful for the cause of Christian unity, but it was not based on mere jealous cantankerousness but on a desire to preserve the spiritual freedom of his Church.

Faced by such opposition the Emperor let the project drop. But he still sought for occasions to please the Papacy. He had many other difficulties with his Church, owing to his eager but usually ill-advised and ill-informed intervention in theological disputes. Towards the end of his reign he had a controversy with the Patriarch over the form of oath to be administered to Christian converts from Islam, as he wished to alter the formula to make it less drastic for the converts. In fact the whole controversy was somewhat pointless as it was based on a mistranslation of a passage from the Koran. In the course of the quarrel Manuel suggested that it should be referred to Rome for arbitration. As he must have known the temper of his bishops by then, one can only assume that he was deliberately teasing them in a manner that they must have thought in questionable taste.[1]

The diplomatic exchanges between the Popes and the three great Emperors of the Comnenian dynasty produced small and evanescent results. The religious debates that they encouraged only served to emphasize the impossibility of formally reconciling the Churches on terms that either side could now accept. But the controversies were still conducted in an atmosphere of courtesy and outward goodwill. No one was prepared to admit that a final and irreparable breach had occurred. Unfortunately during these years political events were increasing the animosity felt mutually against each other by the general population of Eastern and Western Christendom. The Greek and Frankish peoples were rapidly moving farther apart.

[1] Nicetas Choniates, *Historia* (Bonn edition), pp. 278–84. See Chalandon, op. cit., pp. 661–3, esp. p. 661, n. 4.

VI

THE GROWTH OF POPULAR ANIMOSITY

IN Italy the interests of the Papacy and the Byzantine Emperors were often so similar that co-operation between the governments of Rome and Constantinople was not difficult to arrange. But goodwill was continually damaged by events farther to the east. The question of Antioch could never be forgotten for long. The refusal of Pope Innocent II in 1139 to let Latins serve in the Emperor John's army should he interfere in the ecclesiastical affairs of Antioch and the Emperor Manuel's introduction of a Greek Patriarch there in 1165 both strained the relations between the Latins and the Greeks; and the enmity that they aroused was not confined to princes, hierarchs, and theologians but was felt by the common people. A still deeper animosity was engendered by the events of the Second Crusade.

Few movements in history have been started with such splendid hopes and have ended in such a humiliating failure as the Second Crusade. It was preached by Saint Bernard of Clairvaux, the greatest figure of his time in the West. The kings of France and Germany each took the Cross and set out at the head of a great army. But folly and jealousy marred every stage of its course. While the Crusaders were assembling for the journey in 1147 the Emperor Manuel, who had been at war with the Turks, suddenly accepted the offer of a truce made by the Sultan. For so doing he was at once denounced by all the West as a traitor to Christendom. In fact, though he certainly wished to have his hands free while the Crusaders were marching through his lands, it was also necessary for him to prepare the Empire against an attack by Roger of Sicily which he knew to be imminent. Sicilian troops indeed invaded Greece in the summer of

1147; and, though the Pope was distressed by this aggression against the Empire, Western public opinion never paused to consider the effect of King Roger's treachery to the Christian cause.[1] When the German army, led by King Conrad, entered the Balkan provinces of the Empire it at once began to indulge in riots and raids. The native Christians retaliated; and when some local brigands slew a German lord who lingered behind the main army the king's nephew Frederick, the future Emperor Barbarossa, burnt down the nearest monastery and slaughtered the monks, an action ill becoming a prince who prided himself on his Christian piety.[2] The French army, following close behind the German, found that the stores of food which Manuel had prepared had almost entirely been devoured by the Germans, while the natives were grown suspicious and hostile; for which they blamed the Byzantine government more than they blamed the Germans.[3] Manuel vainly tried to persuade both armies to cross over the Hellespont into Asia and so to keep them from approaching Constantinople. Both armies were furious, as everyone wished to visit the great city and its relics. Both armies pillaged the suburbs of Constantinople, though Manuel succeeded in pushing the Germans across the Bosphorus before the French arrived. The temper of the French was so bad by then

[1] See Chalandon, *Les Comnène, Jean II Comnène et Manuel I Comnène*, pp. 257–9, 317–18. It seems that when Manuel thought that only the French were coming on the Crusade he planned a joint expedition with them against the Turks, but when he heard that the Germans were coming too he preferred to keep his hands free (Cinnamus, *Epitome Historiarum*, Bonn edition, p. 59). He made peace with the Turks in the spring of 1147, and Roger's attack began in the spring or summer (Chalandon, op. cit., p. 318, n. 1) at a time when the Greek islands and mainland were denuded of troops. Eudes of Deuil, *De Profectione Ludovici VII in Orientem*, ed. Waquet, p. 53, mentions Roger's attack without any realization of its effect on Manuel's policy. See also Norden, *Das Papsttum und Byzanz*, pp. 81–84.

[2] Cinnamus, op. cit., p. 71; Nicetas Choniates, *Historia* (Bonn edition, p. 85).

[3] Eudes of Deuil, op. cit., pp. 35–44.

that many of them, led by the Bishop of Langres, a cousin of Saint Bernard, urged their king to attack the city; and it was only the influence of the Bishop of Lisieux, a broad-minded and rather irreligious humanist scholar, that dissuaded him.[1] The Germans blandly disregarded Manuel's good advice about strategy and plunged into the centre of Anatolia, to be routed by the Turks near Dorylaeum. The survivors then joined up with the French, except for some pilgrims who insisted on following another route against which the Byzantines had warned them, and suffered terribly on their journey. The French and the rest of the Germans then took Manuel's advice and kept to a road along the coast, but only as far as Ephesus, where Conrad, who was ill, left the army to return to Constantinople and to continue his way to Palestine by sea. At Ephesus King Louis received letters from Manuel telling him that the Turks were on the war-path and begging him to keep within the perimeter of the Byzantine frontier-fortresses. But he insisted on forcing his way through Turkish-controlled territory, where he found the Christian population far better disposed towards the Turks than towards the Franks. After an arduous march the Crusaders reached the port of Attalia. Though it was now midwinter they were furious because the local governor, a man of Latin birth called Landolph, could not at once provide them with enough ships to take them on by sea. The few that were available were snatched by King Louis, his staff, and his senior officers. The rank and file, left leaderless, refused to stay in the camp provided for them by Landolph or even to accept guides from him, but set off on the difficult journey by land to Syria.[2] Not many of them arrived there. In Pales-

[1] Eudes of Deuil, op. cit., pp. 45–48.

[2] Cinnamus, op. cit., pp. 80–86; Eudes of Deuil, op. cit., pp. 53–80; letter of Conrad in *Epistolae Wibaldi*, ed. Jaffé, pp. 152–3; Louis VII, letters to Suger, *R.H.F.*, vol. xv, pp. 488, 495–6. See Runciman, *History of the Crusades*, ii, pp. 267–74.

tine itself the Crusade achieved nothing; and its disasters only added to the general bitterness of the Crusaders.

King Conrad revisited Constantinople on his homeward journey and was delighted by his reception by the Emperor. While he was there a treaty of alliance was signed, and his half-brother, Henry of Austria, married the Emperor's niece. The Byzantines regarded the marriage as a *mésalliance*, and the bride's mother received many expressions of condolence, one of the court poets calling the bridegroom the 'wild beast of the West'.[1] Nor did many of the Germans share their monarch's enthusiasm for Byzantium. His nephew Frederick never forgave the Byzantines for their unfriendliness and for what he thought to be their perfidy. Meanwhile the French and their king were openly hostile. Louis had sailed from Palestine with a Sicilian squadron. Byzantium was still at war with Sicily; and a Byzantine fleet attacked the squadron and captured some of the ships, including one which was carrying most of Louis's luggage. Many months passed before he was able to recover his goods. This was the final outrage.[2] When the French returned home they blamed Byzantium for nearly all their disasters. Their propaganda was effective, and it won the influential support of Saint Bernard. Bernard could not believe that the great Crusade which he had preached could have failed unless sinister forces had intervened. When Louis declared that the villains were the Byzantines, he eagerly agreed, in company with Suger of Saint-Denis and Peter the Venerable of Cluny, who twenty-five years before had written such friendly letters to the Byzantine Emperor

[1] See Chalandon, op. cit., pp. 326–7. Prodromus wrote one poem celebrating the marriage (*R.H.C.Grecs*, vol. ii, p. 772) and another condoling with the bride's mother (ibid., p. 768).

[2] Cinnamus, op. cit., p. 87; letter of Suger, *Sugeri Opera*, ed. de la Marche, pp. 258–60; William of Nangis, *Gesta Ludovici VII*, *R.H.F.*, vol. xx, p. 46. The ship in which Queen Eleanor of France was sailing was detained for a while by the Byzantines (John of Salisbury, *Historia Pontificalis*, ed. Lane-Poole, p. 61).

and Patriarch. The papal legate in Germany, Cardinal Theudwin, joined with them in seeking preachers to launch a Crusade against Constantinople. But the Pope, Eugenius III, was wiser than they and would not encourage them, while King Conrad refused to have anything to do with the movement. But that men of the calibre of Saint Bernard and Peter the Venerable should contemplate a Holy War against Byzantium was ominous for the future peace of the Church.[1]

The whole episode of the Second Crusade marked an important and disastrous turning-point in the relations between the peoples of Western and Eastern Christendom. The Westerners returned thinking that the Byzantines had been treacherous and disloyal to the Faith. They resented the arrogant power and wealth of the Emperor, who seemed to be doing so little to further the Christian cause, by which they meant their cause. He was in relations with the Infidel; he was unfriendly to the Christian princes of Antioch; he had allowed his people to show the Crusade a marked lack of consideration and co-operation. It began to shock the West that the precious relics kept at Constantinople should be in the hands of such un-Christian owners. It was after the Second Crusade that the ordinary Westerner began to regard the East Christian as being something less than a fellow Christian. To the Byzantines the Second Crusade had merely shown the Westerners to be even more savage, unruly, and unreliable than they had previously realized. How could they possibly allow their great and holy Church to submit itself to the domination of a bishop belonging to such a people? The claims of Rome seemed to them more than ever to be preposterous and insolent.

It was noticeable that Frankish colonists settled in the East took a less hostile view of Byzantium than their cousins in western Europe. Princes and noblemen from Outremer

[1] For this project of a Crusade against Byzantium see Bernhardi, *Konrad III*, pp. 810–14; Vacandard, *Vie de Saint Bernard*, ii, pp. 425–8; Norden, *Das Papsttum und Byzanz*, pp. 44–46.

often paid visits to Constantinople and had many friends there. The great historian William of Tyre, though he disapproved at times of Byzantine political actions, showed no particular prejudice against the Byzantine people and had a deep admiration for the Emperor Manuel.[1] So long as Manuel lived, the Courts of Constantinople and Jerusalem were on excellent terms; and even the fiasco of the joint Byzantine-Frankish expedition to Egypt in 1169 did not seriously impair their alliance.

Manuel's death in 1180 marked a second turning-point in the worsening of relations. Though his policy had not always pleased their rulers, Latins had been sure of a personal welcome at his court. He had used his wealth generously in their interests, often himself paying the ransom-money for Crusader princes captured by the Saracens. The Latin Church, even though it resented his intervention at Antioch, could not doubt his genuine desire for a religious understanding. By the strength of his personality he had kept his own people under control. But he had not been a good Emperor. The extravagance of his ambitions had wasted the resources of the Empire, whose economic decline he had refused to realize. In 1176 he had by his own unwisdom led the great Imperial army to disaster at Myriokephalon at the hands of the Turks; and the Byzantine military machine never recovered from the shock. His love of the Latins created increasing resentment in Constantinople and the provinces. All the best posts in the army and the administration seemed to be passing into Frankish hands. Aided by his favour and by their ability to extort political blackmail, the Italian cities were acquiring a

[1] William of Tyre twice went on an embassy to Manuel's Court and was much impressed by the Emperor, at whose death he grieved sincerely (William of Tyre, *Historia*, xx. 4, xxii. 4, 5, *R.H.C.Occ.*, vol. i, pp. 945–7, 1066–9). Manuel was much admired for his readiness to pay the ransom-money for Crusaders captured by the Moslems, e.g. Baldwin of Ibelin. Ernoul, *Chronique d'Ernoul et de Bernard le Trésorier*, ed. Mas Latrie, pp. 56–59.

stranglehold on the trade of the Empire; and the prosperity and arrogance of their merchants infuriated the Greeks whose livelihood was being spoilt. With the removal of his splendid figure the pent-up feelings of the Greeks began to find expression.[1]

Manuel had married twice. His first wife, a German princess, had died leaving him with one daughter, the Caesarissa Maria the Porphyrogennete, whom he married to an Italian prince, Rainier of Montferrat. His second wife, the Latin princess Maria of Antioch, bore him a son, Alexius II, who now succeeded to the throne, at the age of twelve, with the Dowager Empress Maria as regent. Her beauty and charm were admired even by the Greeks; and all the gallants at the court tried to secure her favour. Most unwisely she accepted as her mentor and her lover one of the least capable of her late husband's cousins, the Protosebastos Alexius Comnenus. He was personally unpopular in Constantinople; and his success with the Empress added to the number of his enemies. Maria was naturally inclined to depend upon Manuel's Latin friends; and her lover's unpopularity with his compatriots made him, too, find his supporters amongst the Latins. To the irritated Byzantines it seemed that the whole government of the Empire had passed into Latin hands; and it was easy for the opponents of the Empress to work up the feelings of the populace against these alien masters. In fact, the leaders of the opposition were themselves largely Latin. They were headed by the young Emperor's half-sister, the Caesarissa, and her Italian husband. After a little more than a year of government by the 'foreign woman', as the Greeks called the Empress-Regent, the Caesarissa, counting on the support of anti-Latin feeling in the capital, organized a plot to depose her. The conspiracy was betrayed too soon; and the chief conspirators fled for refuge to the cathedral of Saint Sophia,

[1] For Manuel's concessions to the Italian cities see Heyd, *Histoire du Commerce du Levant*, trans. Furcy Raynaud, 1936 edition, i, pp. 198–222.

knowing that they had the sympathy of the Patriarch and the clergy. The Empress and the Protosebastos sent a company of Latin soldiers to arrest them, but they were unable to force their way into the building. The government was forced by public opinion to offer the Caesarissa and her husband a free pardon. The Empress then tried to depose the Patriarch, Theodosius, banishing him to a monastery, from which he was carried back in triumph by the populace. It was only by the use of her Latin troops that she was able to keep any order in the city. Meanwhile she appealed to her brother-in-law, the King of Hungary, for help.[1]

The Empress-Regent's growing difficulties were being watched with interest by another relative of the late Emperor, Andronicus Comnenus, a man whose youth had been made glamorous by a series of romantic and irresponsible love-affairs and who was now living in retirement and disgrace in Anatolia. He sent a stream of agents to Constantinople to fan the anti-Latin resentment there and to whisper that he alone could save the Empire from the Westerners. In the spring of 1182 he set out to march across Anatolia, and discontented Greeks joined him from every side. In May he was encamped at Chalcedon, on the Asiatic coast opposite to the capital. On the news of his arrival there the whole of Constantinople rose in riot and began to attack the quarters inhabited by the Latins. There followed a ghastly massacre of Franks and Italians, which only ceased when Andronicus unhurryingly crossed into the city and took over the government.[2]

The massacre of the Latins at Constantinople was something that the West could not forgive. It is possible that its horrors have been exaggerated by historians. The only detailed contemporary account is that given by William of

[1] For the history of Alexius II's reign see Ostrogorsky, *Geschichte des byzantinischen Staates*, pp. 314–16. The chief original source is Nicetas Choniates, op. cit., pp. 291–355.

[2] Ostrogorsky, loc. cit.; Nicetas Choniates, op. cit., pp. 325–6; William of Tyre, *Historia*, xxii. 10–11, *R.H.C.Occ.*, vol. i, pp. 1079–82.

Tyre, who wrote at a considerable distance; and the story doubtless lost nothing in its journey to Palestine. The Greek historians pass quickly over the episode, though they saw that it was ominous. Venetian sources make no mention of it at all. Genoese and Pisan sources only mention it briefly, though the Pisans seem to have suffered the most. Indeed, the only sign that the Italians took the massacre seriously was the size of the compensation that they subsequently demanded. Only one Papal Bull refers in passing to the 'persecution' of the Latins. It would probably therefore be wrong to accept every word of William's account, which pictures the angry mob rushing through hospital wards, slaying the patients in their beds and not sparing a single woman or child that it encountered. But, even if we allow for exaggeration, we must admit that many lives were lost, including that of the papal legate and the chaplain of the Pisan colony, and a vast amount of property was destroyed, including all the Latin churches. The massacre was certainly not as wholesale nor as brutal as that conducted by the Crusaders when they captured Jerusalem from the Moslems, or as the long raid on the Christian island of Cyprus made by Reynald of Châtillon. But it was more alarming; for it did not occur on the aftermath of a military victory nor was it a deliberate campaign out for plunder: it was a spontaneous popular movement which took place in the very capital of Eastern Christendom against officially peaceful colonists settled in the city, who suffered simply because they belonged to a Latin race. It seemed to the West to justify the past preaching of the Holy War against Byzantium. It was forgotten that such preaching had helped to provoke the riots, and that they were the reaction of a proud and angry people against a government that seemed to be in the power of unfriendly aliens.[1]

Some fifty Latin ships that were in the harbour of Constantinople managed to sail away, laden with refugees,

[1] See Heyd, op. cit. i, pp. 222–4.

soldiers, and merchants, who took immediate revenge by sacking the islands of the Marmora and the towns along the Thracian coast. Meanwhile Andronicus Comnenus restored order in the capital. The Empress-Regent was thrown into prison, and her young son was soon obliged to sign her death-warrant. Her lover, the Protosebastos, was put to death at the same time. The Caesarissa Maria and her husband soon followed them to the grave. Andronicus became successively regent and co-Emperor; and after a year he quietly had his young cousin killed and was left alone on the throne. This series of murders shocked many of his former supporters. The Patriarch Theodosius threatened to refuse him communion. But Andronicus still enjoyed the favour of the populace. The Patriarch was deposed without difficulty and was replaced by an insignificant cleric called Basil, who did whatever his master ordered.[1]

The new Emperor was a curious man who combined a ruthless and unscrupulous ambition with high political ideals. He made drastic attempts to purge the civil service of inefficiency and corruption. His tax-collectors were honest men; his officials protected the poor against exploitation. Under his rule the peasants in the provinces enjoyed a brief moment of security and prosperity. But he never felt secure in Constantinople, where his cruelty and his harsh autocracy increased the number of his enemies. He had won the throne as champion against the Latins; but as Emperor he soon found it wise to reverse his policy. Latin churches were rebuilt and reopened; Latin merchants were encouraged to return. The Venetian colonies seem to have carried on almost without interruption; and in provincial cities, such as Thessalonica, the Italians had not been disturbed. But Genoa and Pisa demanded redress for their losses, and while on the one hand they sent the Emperor claims for compensation for their losses at Constantinople, on the other they stirred up the powers of western Europe

[1] Nicetas Choniates, op. cit., pp. 343–55. See Ostrogorsky, loc. cit.

against him. His policy of appeasement did him little good. The Papacy broke off relations with Constantinople. The Emperor Frederick Barbarossa, who believed that there should only be one Emperor in Christendom, himself, and one Church, directed by his servant the Pope, was eager to encourage an expedition against Byzantium. But, though his Italian policy had recently been crowned by success at the Peace of Constance, his relations with the Pope were worsening too fast for either to venture upon action in the East. The King of Hungary made a demonstration on the Danube frontier. The only ruler to launch an actual campaign against Andronicus was William II of Sicily. One of the princes of the Comnenian family, called, like so many of his cousins, Alexius, fled to his court and encouraged him against the Emperor. He was soon followed by a boy who claimed, falsely, to be the young Emperor Alexius himself, whom Andronicus had murdered. Making use of the impostor to justify his aggression, William sent his forces eastward in the spring of 1185. In August his generals suddenly pounced on the city of Thessalonica and, after a short siege, in which they were helped by the Italian merchants resident in the city, they forced an entrance. Using Thessalonica as its base, the Norman–Sicilian army prepared to march on Constantinople.[1]

In Constantinople the Emperor's popularity was on the wane. He had grown nervous and suspicious of everyone and began to make arrests and order executions with such wholesale cruelty that public opinion was outraged. The Latin merchants were beginning to return under his patronage, to the irritation of the Greeks; and the news of the loss of Thessalonica and the enemy's advance on the capital brought down his régime. In September he attempted to arrest a respectable elderly nobleman, his cousin Isaac Angelus. Isaac had time to flee for refuge to

[1] For the reign of Andronicus see Ostrogorsky, op. cit., pp. 316–19; Vasiliev, *History of the Byzantine Empire*, pp. 379, 433–8.

Saint Sophia. When the Emperor's guard tried to follow him there, the populace broke out in revolt and stormed the palace. Andronicus was captured and tortured horribly to death; and Isaac Angelus, somewhat to his surprise, found himself raised to the Imperial throne.[1]

Isaac's reign opened with a brilliant military success. His general Branas routed the Normans and recaptured Thessalonica. But this was the Emperor's only triumph. He at once opened negotiations with the West. The Venetians became his allies against the Normans, in return for the promise of new trading-privileges. The Genoese and Pisans, after long bargaining, received compensation for their losses in 1182.[2] Contact was made with Rome, and there was fresh talk of reconciliation between the Churches.[3] But Isaac's attempt to make friends with the West was hindered by his Eastern policy. In order to gain support against the Turks he sought the alliance of Saladin, the arch-enemy of the Crusaders; and this alliance was thought by the Franks to be yet another example of Byzantine perfidy. When Saladin captured Jerusalem in 1187 Isaac at once obtained permission to reinstall the Greek Patriarch in the Holy City.[4] He cannot be blamed for it; it was his Orthodox duty to see that the Christians in the lands newly conquered by the Moslems were not left without an ecclesiastical organization. But he thereby further enraged the Latins. Finally Isaac had to deal with the passage of a great Crusading army, led by Frederick Barbarossa, through his dominions in 1189. Frederick had long disliked Byzantium and openly talked of taking its capital by storm. His army was far better disciplined than any previous Crusading army, and, though

[1] Nicetas Choniates, op. cit., pp. 444–63.

[2] Heyd, op. cit. i, pp. 225–30. The various Chrysobulls in favour of the Italians are given in Dölger, *Regesten*, Nos. 1576–8, 1583, 1589–90, 1606, 1607, 1610, 1616, 1618, ii, pp. 93–95, 97–101.

[3] Dölger, *Regesten*, No. 1615, ii, p. 100, telling of an Imperial embassy to Pope Celestine III, of which no details are known.

[4] See above, p. 91.

it indulged in fewer raids, it was more formidable. Isaac's attempt to put pressure on Frederick by holding his ambassadors as hostages had an effect opposite to that which he had intended. Had Frederick not been anxious to hurry on to Palestine as quickly as possible there might have been a serious clash. When Isaac apologized the Germans agreed to cross into Asia over the Dardanelles; and Constantinople was spared their visit.[1]

Within the Empire Isaac's reign was disastrous. Unfair and excessive taxation provoked a rebellion in Serbia and in Bulgaria, neither of which could be suppressed; and soon the whole interior of the Balkan peninsula was lost. A cousin of the Emperor's, Isaac Ducas Comnenus, governor of Cyprus, declared himself independent Emperor and defeated the attempts of the central government to restore his obedience. Meanwhile the Turks increased their territory in Anatolia at the Empire's expense.[2]

Two years after Frederick Barbarossa's passage through Byzantium relations between Eastern and Western Christendom were far more seriously damaged by the capture of the island of Cyprus by King Richard of England. It may not have grieved Isaac Angelus at the moment to see the elimination of his hated rival, the self-styled Emperor Isaac Comnenus.[3] But the establishment

[1] Nicetas Choniates, op. cit., pp. 525–37; Ansbert, *Expeditio Friderici Imperatoris*, in Chroust, *Quellen zur Geschichte des Kreuzzüges Kaiser Friedrichs I, M.G.H.Ss.*, new series (1928), pp. 27–66; letter of Frederick I to King Henry, in Bohmer, *Acta Imperii Selecta*, p. 152. Frederick declares that the Patriarch publicly preached in Saint Sophia a sermon encouraging the Greeks to kill Westerners. He wishes the Pope to be informed of it.

[2] Ostrogorsky, op. cit., pp. 323–8; Hill, *History of Cyprus*, i, pp. 313–14.

[3] Hill, op. cit. i, pp. 315–21. Nicetas Choniates, op. cit., pp. 547–8, refers to the conquest of Cyprus briefly, with some relish at the fall of Isaac Comnenus. The locally written *De Calamitatibus Cypri* by Neophytus (published in preface to *Itinerarium Regis Ricardi* (ed. Stubbs, Rolls Series), pp. clxxxv–clxxxix) regrets the Latin conquest but rejoices in Isaac's fall.

of a Latin State in Cyprus meant the subordination of the Greek clergy there to Latin new-comers. It was not as in Palestine a century before, where the Greek bishops were all in exile and the sees were in fact, if not in theory, vacant, and where the native Christian population was not Greek. In Cyprus the Greek episcopate was degraded and ordered, with its congregations, to obey alien masters. The history of the struggle between the Churches in Cyprus lies outside of our limits; but it was a constant source of bitterness and anger. In about 1230 thirteen Greek priests were even put to death for refusing to accept the authority of the Roman Church. In the course of the following century the Greeks in Cyprus were forced to accept the status of a Uniate Church, but they never willingly accepted this solution, which they thought humiliating and unjust. As soon as the Turkish conquest in the sixteenth century removed their Latin masters, any pretence of obedience to Rome was shaken off.[1]

In Byzantium itself Isaac Angelus tried to strengthen his position by keeping a tight control over the ecclesiastical hierarchy. He appointed nonentities to the patriarchal throne and forbade them to do anything that might cause an open breach with Rome. He permitted and encouraged Latin churches to hold their services throughout his Empire. He himself married a Latin wife, Margaret of Hungary.[2] But there were still many distinguished and active prelates in the Byzantine Church. A controversy over the question of the corruptibility of the Eucharist produced a mass of theological writing, much of which was of a high calibre. Eustathius, Archbishop of Thessalonica, who died in about 1195, was one of the most learned and

[1] Hill, op. cit. ii, pp. 45–47, iii, pp. 1041–1104. The martyrdom of the Greek priests in Cyprus is the subject of a narrative published in Sathas, *Μεσαιωνικὴ Βιβλιοθήκη*, vol. ii, pp. 20–39.

[2] Heyd, op. cit. i, p. 225. The Venetians were certainly allowed a church, and almost certainly the Genoese and Pisans also: Nicetas Choniates, op. cit., p. 481.

liberal-minded scholars of the century.[1] His pupil, Michael Acominatus Choniates, brother of the historian Nicetas and himself Archbishop of Athens from 1175 to 1205, was a man of enormous culture, with the added attraction of being almost the only important Byzantine writer to use a simple and direct literary style.[2] Such men were not prepared to subordinate themselves to any Westerner. Eustathius had witnessed the Norman sack of Thessalonica in 1185. Michael was to be ejected by the Latins in 1205. More fatally still for the chances of ecclesiastical reconciliation, the Byzantine Church now produced one of its few great lawyers, Theodore Balsamon. Balsamon issued a compendium of Greek canon law and was, even in his lifetime, the authority to whom everyone in the Orthodox world appealed for enlightenment on legal matters. He was appointed Patriarch of Antioch; but the Latins were in possession of the Patriarchate and his title remained nominal. He had therefore a personal grievance against the Latins.

If one wishes to find a villain on the Orthodox side for the development of the schism, Balsamon is a far stronger candidate than either Photius or Cerularius. Hitherto the chief asset of the Orthodox in the controversy had been their doctrine of Economy, the charity that enabled them to overlook and even to condone divergences in the interest of peace and goodwill. But Balsamon was a lawyer; and lawyers like things to be cut and dried. Charity is not one of their characteristics.

Balsamon's general views of the relations of Church and State were completely opposed to those now held at Rome. He accepted the rather vague statements to be found in earlier Byzantine law-books that the Emperor and the

[1] For Eustathius see L. Cohn, article 'Eustathios, Erzbischof von Thessalonike', in Pauly–Wissowa, *Real-Encyclopädie der classischen Altertumswissenschaft*, new edition, vol. xi, coll. 1452–89.

[2] For Michael Choniates see Stadtmüller, 'Michael Choniates, Metropolit von Athen', *Orientalia Christiana*, vol. xxxiii. 2.

Patriarch were the two chief organs of the Empire and that harmony between them was essential. But he maintained that the Emperor must be superior because he was concerned with bodily as well as spiritual affairs, whereas the Patriarch was concerned with spiritual affairs alone. The Emperor, he says, is subject neither to the laws nor to the canons; but he is subject to the doctrines of the Christian Faith, the Faith of the Seven Councils. The deduction to be made from this is that the Emperor is superior to the Pope but also that, for all his power, he was not entitled to bring the Byzantine Church under Rome; for in so doing he would flout the decrees of the Seven Councils, which, so the Byzantines believed, had ordained the Pentarchy of Patriarchs and had issued the divinely inspired Nicene Creed, to which Rome had illegally added a word.[1]

With regard to the Latin Church Balsamon's views were clear and uncompromising. When the Patriarch Mark of Alexandria wrote to ask whether he was right to allow his clergy to give communion to Latins, Balsamon had no doubts about the answer.

> For many years [he wrote in reply] the Western Church has been divided in spiritual communion from the other four Patriarchates and has become alien to the Orthodox, . . . and therefore the Pope is not mentioned in commemoration on the diptychs. So no Latin should be communicated unless he first declares that he will abstain from the doctrines and customs that separate him from us, and that he will be subject to the Canons of the Church, in union with the Orthodox.

He does not demand that Latins should be rebaptized. They are not in the same category as such heretics as the Jacobites or the Nestorians. But he certainly considers that a schism has already taken place, and he implies that it

[1] Theodore Balsamon, *In Canonem XVI Concilii Carthaginiensis*, *M.P.G.*, vol. cxxxviii, col. 93.

occurred when the Pope's name was removed from the diptychs of Constantinople. But he does not say whether he believed therefore that the Churches had been in schism since 1009, nor does he mention the Synod of 1089 which stated that the Pope's name had been removed through carelessness. In his opinion Rome had at some moment lapsed from the correct faith and therefore her bishops could not be commemorated.[1]

Balsamon's high reputation gave authority to his view, which must have been shared by large numbers of Byzantines; and his influence increased with the passage of time and the later trend of events, till it came to be generally accepted that the schism existed in his day. But in fact his attitude was criticized by several of his contemporaries. Demetrius Chomateanus, writing some twenty years later, says that many people at the time thought that he showed too much severity and bitterness, and that he was unjustified in excommunicating the Latins for their forms and usages. None of their practices had been condemned synodically, nor had the Latins ever been labelled as heretics. On the contrary, it was usual for them to feast with the Orthodox and to pray with them.[2] That is to say, there were large sections of the Byzantine population that believed that though there might be quarrels between the hierarchs the congregations of East and West were still in full communion.

On the Latin side it seems that by the close of the century the Greeks were generally held to be schismatic. The lawyers at Rome inevitably considered that the refusal of the Orthodox to admit Roman supremacy constituted a declaration of schism. Public opinion no longer, as at the time of the First Crusade, regarded Constantinople as a holy city. When after the Fourth Crusade the citizens of

[1] Theodore Balsamon, letter to Mark of Alexandria, *M.P.G.*, vol. cxxxviii, col. 968.

[2] Demetrius Chomateanus, letter, *M.P.G.*, vol. cxix, coll. 956–60.

Angers received relics stolen from Byzantium they sang in their hymn of welcome the words:

> Constantinopolitana
> Civitas diu profana. . . .
>
> City of Constantinople
> Which has been so long ungodly. . . .[1]

But, as with the Greeks, no one could state how long the schismatic ungodliness had been in existence. At the same time, in all Villehardouin's account of the Fourth Crusade there is no suggestion that the Greeks are not fellow Christians. 'You are Christians and we are Christians', said the Emperor Alexius III to the Crusaders, and they did not contradict him.[2] The expedition was not planned *contra schismaticos* but as a legitimate attempt to place the rightful claimant on the Byzantine throne. But when the Crusaders stated their terms to the Emperor, the first was that he must place the whole Empire of Romania under the obedience of Rome, 'from which it has in the past separated itself'.[3] The attitude of the West seems to have been that all that was required of the Eastern Churches was their submission to the Pope, against whom they had rebelled at some unspecified date in the past.

Meanwhile the courts of Rome and Constantinople remained in communication with each other. The Emperor Isaac Angelus was dethroned in 1195 in a palace revolution. He was blinded and imprisoned; and his brother Alexius took his place. Isaac fell largely because of the compensation that he gave to the Italians in amends for the riots of 1182, which was too generous for Byzantine

[1] *Sequentia Andegavensis*, in Riant, *Exuviae Sacrae Constantinopolitanae*, vol. ii, p. 45.

[2] Villehardouin, *La Conquête de Constantinople*, ed. Faral, i, p. 144.

[3] Ibid. ii, p. 24 (the clergy tell the Crusaders that the Pope will be pleased if Constantinople is forced to return to his obedience); Letter of Baldwin of Flanders, *R.H.F.*, vol. xviii, p. 522.

tastes.[1] Alexius Angelus therefore began his reign as a champion against the Latins. But he soon found it necessary to open negotiations with the Pope. The Western Emperor Henry VI, Barbarossa's son, conquered his wife's heritage of Sicily in 1194. Both from his father and from his wife's Norman ancestors he inherited an ambition to conquer Byzantium. Henry's multifarious ambition was equally alarming to the Papacy, which could not afford to allow any increase in his power. Their mutual interests drew the Emperor Alexius and Pope Celestine III together; and though no definite alliance was concluded, it is probable that their *entente* did to some extent check Henry's schemes.[2] Henry's unexpected death in 1197 eased the situation. But his successor in Germany, his brother Philip of Swabia, though less powerful was almost as ambitious; and he had a personal feud with Alexius, having married the daughter of the dispossessed Emperor Isaac. When Celestine was succeeded by Innocent III in 1198, Alexius wrote to congratulate the new Pope and to urge a political alliance.[3]

Innocent was in a stronger position than Celestine had been. He was guardian of Henry's young son, Frederick of Sicily, and he had roused opposition against Philip of Swabia in Germany. So, though he welcomed the Emperor's overtures, he replied that it would be rather difficult for him to ally himself with a prince whose Church did not recognize the supremacy of the Holy See. His ambassadors told the Emperor that his first duty was to bring back the daughter-Church of Constantinople to its mother of Rome, and also to promise to take part in a Crusade against the infidel.[4] Alexius answered cautiously. He would gladly

[1] Heyd, op. cit. i, p. 226. The revolt of Branas, inspired by anti-Italian feeling, had been brutally suppressed by Isaac's Latin mercenaries led by Conrad of Montferrat. Nicetas Choniates, op. cit., pp. 502–10.

[2] Norden, op. cit., pp. 130–3; Dölger, *Regesten*, No. 1635, ii, p. 103.

[3] Ibid., No. 1643, ii, p. 104.

[4] Innocent III's letter, i. 353, *M.P.L.*, vol. ccxiv, col. 327.

support a Crusade and would even give his life for it, but on his side it was rather difficult for him to ally himself with the Latins in the East who had unrighteously stolen his island of Cyprus. As for the union of the Churches, that could easily be achieved if 'human wishes would subordinate themselves to the Divine wish', that is to say, if a General Council were summoned, to which the Holy Ghost would provide inspiration. The Church of Constantinople would willingly send plenipotentiaries to such a council.[1] A reply was also sent to the Pope by the Patriarch, John Camaterus, who had recently been raised to the throne of Constantinople through the influence of his cousin, the Empress Euphrosyne, but who was a more forceful and reputable person than his immediate predecessors. He expressed surprise at the claim of Rome to be the mother-Church of Christendom. Surely, he commented, if we give any Church that title, it should be the Church of Jerusalem, where Christ founded the Church. He added that if anyone was rending the tunic of Christ it was Rome, who having signed the acts of Nicaea was altering the Nicene Creed.[2]

Innocent's patient answer showed that he was still anxious to be friendly. He explained at length to the Patriarch that Rome was the mother-Church, not because of her age but because of her dignity, an argument that had little effect in Constantinople which felt itself to be a city of far greater dignity than Rome. He told the Emperor that he welcomed the idea of a General Council. Indeed he already had one in mind. But before it could be summoned he must insist that Constantinople should admit the supremacy of Rome.[3] Inevitably the negotiations came to a standstill. But the Pope and Emperor continued to send each other

[1] Alexius's letter is quoted in Innocent's letter ii. 210, ibid., coll. 765–8.
[2] The Patriarch's letter is quoted in Innocent's letter, ii. 211, ibid., coll. 768–9.
[3] Innocent III, letter cited above, previous note.

polite messages. Neither wished to abandon the possibility of an alliance, for both were nervous of what Philip of Swabia might do. Innocent, however, gave up any hope of securing active Byzantine help for a Crusade.

The Crusade remained his chief ambition, even taking precedence over the union of the Churches. But the result that his eager efforts produced were to make the union of the Churches for ever impossible.

VII

THE FOURTH CRUSADE

IT was the movement known in history as the Fourth Crusade which brought relations between the Churches of Rome and Constantinople to a crisis. From the moment of his accession Pope Innocent III had sought to launch a new Crusade. He encouraged preachers such as Fulk of Neuilly in France and Martin of Pairis in Germany to tour the country-side and rouse men to their duty. In the autumn of 1199 his hopes seemed near to fruition. That September Count Tybalt of Champagne invited his friends to a tournament at Ecry-sur-Yonne. Fulk of Neuilly suddenly appeared amongst them and spoke to them so eloquently that they all took the Cross. Their example was followed by nobles all over northern France, Lorraine, and Germany.[1] The Pope was delighted; but two unexpected events took the movement out of his control. Tybalt of Champagne had been accepted as leader of the Crusade; but in the spring of 1201 he died, before the Crusaders were ready to set out for the East. In his place, on the suggestion of the French king, they elected as their leader the Marquis Boniface of Montferrat. It seemed a suitable appointment. Boniface was related to both the French and German royal houses. His family had many connexions with the East, where his father had died and his brothers had made their careers; and he himself was a distinguished and experienced soldier. But he was an intimate friend of the Pope's enemy, Philip of Swabia.[2] Secondly, in their need for transport the

[1] Villehardouin, *La Conquête de Constantinople*, ed. Faral, i, pp. 2–6.

[2] Ibid. i, pp. 40–46; Robert of Clary, *La Conquête de Constantinople*, ed. Lauer, pp. 4–6; *Gesta Innocentii III*, *M.P.L.*, vol. ccxiv, col. 132. The *Gesta Innocentii* suggests that the King of France was responsible for Boniface's appointment. Boniface's father had died as a Palestinian baron.

Crusaders decided to hire ships from the Venetians. But the Venetians' terms were high; and soon after the Crusaders had arrived at Venice they found themselves so heavily indebted to their hosts that they were obliged to offer to help the republic on a purely local campaign, to reconquer the city of Zara which had recently been annexed by the King of Hungary. The king was a good Catholic son of the Church; and the Pope was horrified to learn that the first action of the Crusade was to be an attack on a Christian town. His protests were disregarded. In November 1202 the Crusaders and the Venetians set out together to besiege and capture Zara.[1]

While they were there celebrating their victory, excommunicated by the Pope, who soon forgave the Crusaders but not the Venetians, they were joined by a young Byzantine prince, Alexius, son of the dispossessed Emperor Isaac Angelus. He had recently escaped from the confinement in which his uncle Alexius III had kept him and fled to the court of his sister, Philip of Swabia's wife. Philip interested himself in his brother-in-law's cause and evolved with Boniface of Montferrat a plan to use the Crusade to place him on the Byzantine throne. Boniface then approached the Venetian Doge, Andrea Dandolo, who many years before had damaged his sight as the result of a brawl at Constantinople and thereafter hated the Byzantines. The young Alexius promised that as soon as he was installed as Emperor he would provide military aid and large sums of money for the Crusaders and trade-concessions and money for the Venetians. The Pope was not consulted; and when

His eldest brother had been married to the heiress-presumptive of Jerusalem, Sibylla, and their infant son had been King of Jerusalem. His brother Rainier had married the Porphyrogennete Maria and had been murdered at Constantinople by Andronicus (see above, p. 133). His brother Conrad had first been married to a sister of Isaac Angelus, then had gone to Palestine where he saved Tyre from Saladin and married the heiress of Jerusalem, Isabella. Boniface's mother was half-sister to Henry VI's grandfather and his father half-brother to King Philip of France's grandmother.

[1] See Runciman, *History of the Crusades*, iii, pp. 113–15.

he heard rumours of the project he was not pleased. He was not impressed by what he had seen or heard of the young prince, and he wished the Crusade to proceed as quickly as possible to the Holy Land. But he was powerless to stop the diversion. Amongst the Crusaders there were many who shared his view and who left the main army to go at once to Palestine. But most of the knights and soldiers were delighted at the prospect of securing the co-operation of Byzantium for their movement and some of its fabulous wealth for themselves.[1]

In April 1203 the Crusade set sail from Zara, with Alexius, and reached the harbour of Constantinople on 24 June. His uncle, the Emperor Alexius III, had made no preparation to meet the invasion, partly because his information had been faulty and partly because he could not trust either his army or his subjects. But the Crusaders' hope that the pretender would at once be welcomed by the Byzantines as their legitimate sovereign was disappointed. The actual Emperor found himself unexpectedly well supported. The Franks and Venetians therefore attacked the city fortifications, which were vigorously defended. The issue was not a clear one between Latin and Greek. The Genoese and the Pisans held aloof, rightly suspecting Venetian intentions. On the Byzantine side the defence was headed by the regiments of the Imperial Guard, the Varangians, who were recruited at this time from Englishmen and Danes. On 17 July the Venetians made a breach in the walls. The Emperor Alexius III thereupon fled from the city, reflecting with what fortunate results King David had fled before Absalom. The Byzantine officials hastened to bring out from his enforced retirement the blind ex-Emperor Isaac, the pretender's father. This ingenious move obliged the young Alexius to call off his allies' attack. The Crusaders and Venetians agreed to make a truce on the understanding that the pretender should be created joint Emperor with

[1] Ibid., pp. 112 (and n. 2), 115–17.

his father and that he should carry out the promises that he had made to them. He was also to oblige the clergy of the Empire to acknowledge the supremacy of Rome.[1]

The new Emperor Alexius IV found himself quite unable to fulfil these conditions. The Treasury was far emptier than he had thought; he could not possibly give his allies the great sums that they demanded. The Byzantine clergy, led by the Patriarch, flatly refused to support his romanizing policy. There was growing discontent in the city, while the Crusaders were impatient for their rewards. At last Dandolo planned to bring things to a head by adding to the Venetian claims. In January 1204, when his new demands were known, there was a riot in the city which Alexius only just succeeded in quieting. In February the Franks and Venetians sent a delegation to the palace insisting that the promised payments should be made at once. Alexius confessed his impotence, while the delegates were almost torn to pieces by the angry crowd, which rushed on the church of Saint Sophia, where Alexius was declared to be deposed. The leaders of the crowd then offered the throne to an elderly nobleman called Nicholas Canabus, who happened to be saying his prayers in the church. He refused the honour in terror; and the crowd, led now by a son-in-law of Alexius III, Alexius Murzuphlus, poured back to the palace. Alexius IV was seized and thrown into a dungeon, where he was strangled. His father, the old Emperor Isaac, who had spent the last months closeted with astrologers but had derived no comfort from their predictions, was imprisoned once more and died after a few days from grief, helped by ill-treatment. Alexius Murzuphlus meanwhile ascended the throne as Alexius V.[2]

This was a direct challenge to the Crusaders. The Doge now urged the destruction of Byzantium and its replacement by a Latin Empire; and the Crusaders agreed with

[1] See Runciman, *History of the Crusades*, iii, pp. 117–19.
[2] Ibid., pp. 119–21.

him. Throughout March discussions were held in the camp about the future constitution of the new Empire. It was decided that the Emperor should be chosen by six Crusader and six Venetian electors. If a Crusading prince was elected, a Venetian should be nominated as Patriarch. The Emperor should have the Imperial palaces and a quarter of the rest of the city and of the Empire. The remainder should be divided into two halves, one to be allotted to the leading Crusader princes who should hold their lands as fiefs under the Emperor, the other to the Venetians in complete sovereignty. All would thus be arranged, the treaty declared, 'for the honour of God, of the Pope and of the Empire'. The Pope was not consulted.[1]

The Crusaders' second attack on Constantinople began on 6 April 1204. The Emperor Alexius Murzuphlus was short of men and of money. He could not pay the wages of the Varangian Guard, whose members started to desert. Even so, the first assault was driven off; but on 12 April the Venetians made a breach at the point where the land-walls came down to the Golden Horn. The defenders still held the inner wall; but a fire broke out behind them. They were forced to retire, and the whole defence collapsed. Murzuphlus fled out of the city into Thrace, to join his father-in-law. Another of Alexius III's sons-in-law, Theodore Lascaris, tried to rally the garrison and to persuade the Varangians to fight on. But their spirit was broken. While the enemy burst through the city, Lascaris and the Patriarch escaped by sea across to Asia.

The fighting in the streets soon died down. By next morning the Doge and the leading Crusader princes were established in the Great Palace, and their soldiers were told that they could spend the next three days in pillage. The Crusaders' sack of Constantinople is one of the most

[1] Ibid., p. 121. Baldwin's report to the Pope gives the rough text of the Crusaders' decision (letter of Baldwin of Flanders, *R.H.F.*, vol. xviii, p. 522).

ghastly and tragic incidents in history. The Byzantines prided themselves, with justice, on their learning and culture. Now they saw their libraries going up in flames, with all the manuscripts of the ancient world and all their classical and contemporary works of art. More immediately horrifying were the outrages committed on the men, women, and children of the city and on its priests, monks, and nuns. What shocked the godly East most deeply was the sacrilege done to the churches. In Saint Sophia ribald French prostitutes rollicked through the sanctuary. One of them sat herself on the patriarchal throne, where Frankish soldiers paid her mock homage in the intervals of tearing down the silken hangings and pulling to pieces the great silver iconostasis and altar. Not a church was spared. Indeed, the pious Abbot Martin of Pairis congratulated himself on the delicacy of his feelings, which allowed him only to rob religious buildings. How much was wantonly destroyed cannot be known. What survived was taken by the victors. The Venetians, shrewder and better educated than the Franks, managed to rescue and keep for themselves many of the most valuable treasures; and even after all the holocaust the piles of booty were so great that the Crusaders could not believe their eyes. Never, said Villehardouin, had so much loot been taken in any one city. But the price was the lasting enmity of Greek Christendom.[1]

[1] The sack of Constantinople is described on the Greek side by Nicetas Choniates, *Historia* (Bonn edition), pp. 757–63, by Nicholas Mesarites, *Opera*, in Heisenberg, *Neue Quellen zur Geschichte des lateinischen Kaisertums*, i, pp. 41–48; and letter of Greek clergy to Innocent III, in Cotelerius, *Ecclesiae Graecae Monumenta*, iii, pp. 510–14. The Latin descriptions, which are more concerned with the size of the booty and the greed of the Crusaders, are by Villehardouin, op. cit. ii, pp. 52–58; Robert of Clary, op. cit., pp. 68–69, 80–81; Gunther of Pairis, *Historia Constantinopolitana*, in Riant, *Exuviae Sacrae Constantinopolitanae*, i, pp. 104–8; letter of Baldwin of Flanders, *R.H.F.*, vol. xviii, p. 522; Ernoul (*Chronique d'Ernoul et de Bernard le Trésorier*), ed. Mas Latrie, pp. 374–6. The most damning account is that written by Innocent III on reports that he eventually received in his letter viii. 126, *M.P.L.*, vol. ccxv, coll. 699–702. An account from the Greek point of view is given in the *Novgorod*

The Fourth Crusade could never be forgiven nor forgotten by the Christians of the East. Thenceforward there was definite schism between the Greek and Latin Churches. Yet the very disaster of the fall of Constantinople had so demoralizing an effect on the Byzantine world that it offered to the Papacy a supreme opportunity for winning the allegiance of the Greeks. Had Pope Innocent III been a little bit more elastic in his policy he might have secured the submission of the Church of Constantinople. The Pope was in a difficult position. He had not at all approved of the diversion of the Crusade. He was genuinely shocked that soldiers who had vowed to fight the Holy War against the infidel should have turned their arms against a Christian people, even if the people were unwilling to admit his supremacy. But he could not fail to rejoice at the foundation of a Latin Empire which seemed to bring all Byzantium and its Church into the Roman fold. He was pleased that the Emperor whom the victorious soldiers elected was not his enemy, Boniface of Montferrat, but the amiable and pious Count Baldwin of Flanders.[1] Though he deplored the over-prompt election of the Venetian Morosini as Patriarch without reference to himself, yet Morosini, once elected, was properly deferential to the Holy See.[2] When first he heard of the capture of the city and the installation of the Latin Emperor he wrote a warm letter of congratulation to the new Emperor and praised God.[3] But when further information reached him he was less well satisfied. He was shocked and angry to learn that the Crusaders did not now intend to go on to fight in Palestine but meant to

Chronicle, ed. Nasonov (Academy of Sciences of the U.S.S.R.), pp. 245–6.

[1] See below, pp. 153–4.

[2] Innocent cancelled Morosini's appointment and then reappointed him himself. Innocent, letters vii. 203, 204, *M.P.L.*, vol. ccxv, coll. 512–17.

[3] Innocent, letters vii. 153, 154, *M.P.L.*, vol. ccxv, coll. 454–5. He calls the capture of Constantinople *magnifica miracula*.

settle in Byzantine lands and devote their energy and resources to the foundation of colonies there. His horror was increased when he heard details of the sack of Constantinople and all the bloodshed and the sacrilege. No account of those terrible days is more lurid and severe than that which he wrote on the reports that were given to him.[1] But his second reaction came too late. The East only remembered his first expression of delight. Most of the Orthodox were convinced that he had had a hand in the whole affair.[2]

In fact Innocent realized that the creation of the Latin Empire raised grave ecclesiastical problems. A Latin lay aristocracy and a Latin Church hierarchy might be superimposed upon Byzantium, but the population was Greek. The Greek Church could not be simply abolished or even latinized. The Pope decided that the Greek hierarchy must be disturbed as little as possible, so long as it recognized the supremacy of Rome. But many of the Greek bishops refused to accept Latin rule and went into exile. Innocent begged the new Latin authorities not to be too precipitate in filling the vacant sees with Latins. He wished to be as helpful as possible to the Greeks. All that he demanded from their bishops was that they should sign a declaration in which each of them was to promise that:

> I shall henceforward be faithful and obedient to Saint Peter, to the Holy Roman Church, to the Apostolic See, to my lord Innocent and his Catholic successors. I shall defend as far as I can against every living creature the Roman Papacy, its honours, its dignities and its possessions. I shall come to a Council whenever my presence is required. I shall pay a visit *ad limina* [that is to say, to the Papal Court] either personally or by proxy. Finally I shall receive with the respect due to him the Legate of the Apostolic See and shall assist him in everything.[3]

[1] Innocent, letter viii. 126, *M.P.L.*, vol. ccxv, coll. 699–702.

[2] *Novgorod Chronicle*, loc. cit., roundly accuses the Pope of having instigated the Crusade.

[3] Innocent, letter xi. 23, *M.P.L.*, vol. ccxv, col. 1352. In a letter, xi. 24, to Morosini, *M.P.L.*, vol. ccxv, col. 1353, he says that Greek bishops

In addition the bishop must add the names of the Pope and of the Latin Patriarch of Constantinople to the diptychs of his Church.[1]

Unfortunately it was impossible to carry out this conciliatory policy. In the first place the Crusaders failed to conquer the whole Byzantine Empire. Three Greek succession-states appeared, that of Theodore Lascaris and his successors at Nicaea, that of a branch of the Comneni at Trebizond, and that of a branch of the Angeli in Epirus. The Greeks who refused to accept Latin domination had therefore several places of refuge, whence they could carry on anti-Latin propaganda. Many leading Greek bishops, including such respected figures as Michael Acominatus of Athens, left their sees, forced out by the Latins or preferring voluntarily to escape from their rule; and most of them retired to Nicaea.[2] In the second place the Latins were not willing to be conciliatory. Most of the conquering princes were eager to reward their followers and themselves by taking over the best posts and estates, lay and ecclesiastical; nor were they averse from annexing the property of Greek monasteries and bishoprics. Other Latins, such as Boniface of Montferrat, who became King of Thessalonica, and his wife, the ex-Empress Margaret, Isaac Angelus's widow, took the opposite line and, in order to win popular support against their rivals, deliberately supported the Greek clergy against the Latin and encouraged them in their refusal to

who are already consecrated need not be reconsecrated by a Latin rite, but all new consecrations must follow the Latin rite. He gives a similar formula in a letter to the Archbishop of Tirnovo, letter vii. 11, ibid., col. 295.

[1] Innocent, letter xi. 23, loc. cit.

[2] See Gardner, *The Lascarids of Nicaea*, pp. 67, 97–100. For Michael Acominatus see Miller, *The Latins in the Levant*, pp. 34, 71–72. Michael was not too intransigent not to advise the Abbot of Kaisariani to come to terms with the conquerors. The general opinion of the Greek clergy is given in the *Criminationes adversus Ecclesiam Latinam* (published in Cotelerius, *Monumenta Ecclesiae Graecae*, vol. iii, pp. 495 ff.), which was apparently drafted by the clergy of Nicaea soon after 1204.

co-operate.[1] Finally there was the question of the Patriarchate. The Greek Patriarch, John Camaterus, lived on till 1206.[2] He had never resigned; and the election of Morosini was quite uncanonical. Even the Greek bishops who were prepared to compromise with Rome could not bring themselves to acknowledge the Latin intruder. But Innocent could not bring himself to repudiate Morosini. He seems to have thought that a Latin Patriarch was necessary to guarantee the adhesion of the Church of Constantinople to Rome. This was his great mistake.

Innocent's supreme opportunity came in 1206. John Camaterus had recently died, and the Greeks considered the Patriarchate to be vacant. The first Latin Emperor, Baldwin, had disappeared in captivity in a Bulgarian castle; and the new Emperor, his brother Henry, the only statesman that the Latin Empire was to produce, was a man for whom the Greeks as well as the Latins had a real respect. The Greek succession-states were quarrelling with each other; none of them seemed certain of survival. The Greek clerics who had remained within the new Latin Empire met together. They were realists. They saw little hope of the rebirth of the Byzantine Empire and they were ready to accept Henry as their Emperor. They were ready, too, to admit the supremacy of Rome so long as they could keep their old traditions. They drafted a letter to the Pope. They would recognize him, they said, as Pope and Thirteenth Apostle and, at Henry's suggestion, they offered to give to his name the traditional Imperial Acclamation, after the last prayer in the Liturgy. They even declared that their sufferings would have been justified if out of them there

[1] A report of the Archbishop of Patras quoted by Innocent, letter xiii, 161, *M.P.L.*, vol. ccxvi, col. 338, complains of the illegal rapacity of the lay princes. Innocent's letter ix. 189, to the Archbishops of Patras and Thebes and the Bishop of Thermopylae, *M.P.L.*, vol. ccxv, coll. 1467–8, tells them to warn the Empress Margaret against protecting the Greek clergy in the diocese of Larissa.

[2] See Gardner, op. cit., loc. cit.

emerged real union between the Churches. All that they asked was that they should have a Patriarch who shared their language, customs, and traditions. In the past there had been, they said, not quite accurately, two Patriarchs and one Prince in Antioch and Jerusalem; so why not at Constantinople?[1] That is to say, the Greeks asked to be allowed to form a Uniate Church, with its own liturgy and hierarchy, under the overriding authority of Rome. It was a solution that the Papacy was to try out at Antioch some forty years later; but Innocent found it too revolutionary. It had indeed one unsurmountable drawback. The Greek line of Patriarchs would indubitably and rightly be considered to be the legitimate and apostolic line, and the Latins would be recognized as intruders; and in fact the arrangement did not last for long at Antioch. But had Innocent listened to the Greeks' request he might have succeeded in winning the allegiance of the Church of Constantinople. Byzantium was at its lowest ebb. A grand conciliatory gesture on the part of Rome and the emergence of the Pope as champion of the Greeks against the Franks and the Venetians might have persuaded the people of Byzantium to forget their past proud independence, which had been based on the greatness of their Empire. The lead of Constantinople might well have been followed by the provincial Churches. The Greeks would have been divided, and the Latin Empire might have endured.

Innocent, however, left the proposal unanswered. He was not prepared to sacrifice any of the claims of the Latin Patriarch. His lack of sympathy drove the party of reconciliation into the arms of the extremists in exile. The majority of the bishops of the Patriarchate hurried to

[1] The letter of the Greek clergy to Innocent III is given in Cotelerius, op. cit., pp. 514 ff., printed as part of the *Criminationes*, chapter lxxxv onwards. See Luchaire, *Innocent III: La Question d'Orient*, pp. 251–6. It seems that the Greek clergy were supported by the Emperor, Henry, in opposition to the new papal legate, Cardinal Pelagius. The date was 1214.

Nicaea and there elected a Patriarch who was accepted by the Orthodox world.[1] His presence gave new strength to the resistance; and with his support the ruler of Nicaea, Theodore Lascaris, became generally recognized as the lawful Emperor. Even so, the moderates continued to negotiate with the Pope, asking him to summon a General Council. But he insisted that if any such council were called the Church of Constantinople must be represented by delegates appointed by the Latin Patriarch, and not by the Greek at Nicaea. Nor did he make things easier for the Greeks by refusing to Theodore Lascaris any title higher than 'Noble Lord'.[2]

It was the last opportunity. Greek public opinion had never given much support to the policy of compromise. The Greek bishops soon recovered from their moment of despair; and as their spirits rose so did their pride in the great Orthodox tradition, of which they were consciously the heirs. Negotiations between Rome and Byzantium did not abruptly cease. The Pope was far too important a figure in international politics for any ruler, however schismatic, not to wish to keep up some contact with him. Theodore Lascaris's son-in-law and heir, John Vatatzes, tried to divert the ill will that the Papacy showed to the Nicaean Empire by inducing his Patriarch, Germanus II, to enter

[1] See Gardner, op. cit., pp. 97–98. Michael Authoreanus, the new Patriarch, had been acting as Patriarch before Camaterus's death, and his enemies were doubtful about the canonicity of his election, as the bishops of the whole Patriarchate had not been invited to the election and he was nominated by Theodore Lascaris whom he then crowned Emperor.

[2] Negotiations had been going on between the court of Nicaea, Thomas Morosini, and, later, the papal legate Benedict of Saint Susanna. Nicholas Mesarites, Bishop of Ephesus, and Michael Acominatus were both involved. See Heisenberg, *Neue Quellen zur Geschichte des lateinischen Kaisertums und der Kirchenunion*, Pt. II, 'Die Unionsverhandlung vom 30 August, 1206', and Pt. III, 'Der Bericht des Nicolaos Mesarites über die politischen und kirchlichen Ereignisse des Jahres 1214'. See also Norden, op. cit., pp. 215–33. Innocent had written a patronizing and scolding letter to Theodore Lascaris on 17 March 1208 (letter xi. 47, *M.P.L.*, vol. ccxv, col. 1272).

into correspondence with the Pope and eventually to arrange for papal representatives, two Franciscan and two Dominican monks, to visit the Nicaean Court. But the council held at Nymphaeum in 1234 was an utter failure. The Greeks had hoped for a General Council and invited delegates from the Eastern Patriarchates. Euthymius, exiled Greek Patriarch of Antioch, was present. But Pope Gregory IX would not give the discussions so official a status. Pope and Emperor were both willing to make some concessions. Gregory seems to have been prepared to recognize the Patriarch at Nicaea as lawful Patriarch of Constantinople. Vatatzes urged his clergy to accept the Latin thesis on the Eucharist, which maintained that though the Greek use of leavened bread was not wrong, the Latin use of unleavened was more fully symbolical; but he demanded that in return the Latins should omit the *Filioque* from the official Creed. Neither side would make such concessions; and the papal delegates insisted that the first step must be the Greeks' submission to the Holy See. The goodwill in which the conference had been begun soon evaporated. In the end the Latin monks withdrew from the debating-chamber in a rage, while the Greek bishops shouted at them: 'You are heretics. We found you heretics and excommunicates and we leave you heretics and excommunicates.' And the Latins shouted back: 'You are heretics too.'[1]

No one now could deny that the schism was in existence. When the Emperor Frederick II sent his daughter Constance to be the second wife of Vatatzes, he was denounced at Rome for this marriage-alliance with a schismatic.[2] At the Council of Lyons in 1245 Pope Innocent IV announced his concern over the 'schism of Romania, that is, of the Greek Church, which in our own time, only a few years ago,

[1] Hefele–Leclercq, *Histoire des Conciles*, v. 2, pp. 1569–72.

[2] Ibid., p. 1678. This was given as one of the reaons for excommunicating Frederick at the Council of Lyons.

arrogantly and foolishly seceded and removed itself from the bosom of its mother as though she were a step-mother'.[1] Though embassies might still pass between Rome and the courts of the Orthodox East, and though intermarriage might continue between the royal houses of East and West, yet it was an undeniable fact that the Churches were no longer in communion. The accusation of heresy was only made by one side against the other in moments of anger, though to the Orthodox the Roman addition to the Creed seemed to be a repudiation of the Faith of the Seven Councils, and to the Catholics the Greek rejection of the Petrine claims was ultimately to be considered heresy. The distinction between schism and heresy was not always clear. It was tragic enough that the raiment of Christ was torn.

The subsequent history of the schism and of the attempts to mend it lie beyond the scope of this study. Twice the breach was nominally healed; twice the Church of Constantinople officially recognized the supremacy of Rome, at Lyons in 1276 and at Florence in 1439. In both cases the Emperor and his servant the Patriarch genuinely subscribed to the union. But in both cases the prime motive was political; and in neither was the union accepted by more than a tiny minority of the Byzantine clergy or of the Byzantine people. It remained meaningless and soon faded away. The Patriarchates of Antioch and Jerusalem were already in permanent schism with Rome, which maintained a rival line of Latin Patriarchs. The Patriarchate of Alexandria was in schism from the fourteenth century onwards. In Constantinople the failure of the West to rescue Byzantium in its death-agony at the hands of the Turks removed the last possible chance of reconciliation.

[1] Matthew Paris, *Chronica Majora*, ed. Luard (Rolls Series), vol. iv, p. 434.

VIII

THE DATE AND NATURE OF THE SCHISM

AT the beginning of the eleventh century Christendom was still one. Apart from the long-established heretic bodies in the East, the Nestorians and the Monophysites, the great Churches saw themselves as parts of a single Church, coterminous with the world of Christian peoples. By the middle of the thirteenth century the Churches of Eastern and Western Christendom were consciously separated. When and why did the great schism occur?

The date that the world has generally accepted for the schism between Rome and Constantinople is 1054. The quarrel that took place that year between the Patriarch Michael Cerularius and Cardinal Humbert was an ugly and bitter episode in ecclesiastical history which undoubtedly helped in creating an atmosphere of schism; but it was neither the first nor the last episode in the sorry story. Contemporaries assigned a different date for the schism, but few of them agreed over it. The average Greek cleric of today considers that the absence of the Roman bishop's name from the diptychs of the Eastern Churches is the symbol of schism, therein following the view of the lawyer Balsamon. But it is unlikely that Balsamon himself believed that the Churches were in schism ever since the year 1009, when, apparently, Constantinople mentioned a Pope for the last time on its diptychs. The Chartophylax Nicetas indicates that that schism was healed, though he does not say how or when. The Byzantine churchmen of 1089 declared that the Pope's name had been removed carelessly and by mistake. Throughout the period the Eastern

Patriarchs were apt to complain that the Bishop of Rome had separated himself from his brother-Patriarchs by his action in adding to the Creed. But, till Balsamon's time, there is no suggestion that the whole Western Church was considered actually schismatic by the average Greek churchman. The Latins were still more shy of pronouncing the Eastern Churches to be in definite schism. As we have seen, Pope Innocent IV, speaking in 1245, when the schism was an undoubted fact, implies that it had only happened within his lifetime. He probably dated it from 1206, when the Greeks explicitly refused to accept the Latin Patriarch of Constantinople and appointed a Patriarch of their own. But, though the word 'schismatic' might be avoided, Western opinion had long since begun to regard the Greeks as hostile and as false Christians, while Frederick Barbarossa wrote in indignation that the Greeks accused the Latins of being heretical.

It is, in fact, impossible to give a precise date for the schism. This is because of its nature. There are several planes on which it must be considered. The theological issue, which was to produce the largest amount of controversial writing, that is to say, the quarrel over the Procession of the Holy Ghost, was not in itself a cause for schism, any more than divergences of usage in the liturgy. In the earlier days of the Church there had been no insistence on uniformity of ritual; and even after the split had begun to be obvious the saner leaders on either side were prepared to allow that the divergences were permissible. Similarly, the difference of opinion on the Procession of the Holy Ghost represented slightly different views about the Trinity, on a point which was not covered by an Oecumenical Council or any other authoritative doctrinal pronouncement. Mutual tolerance, which was often advocated on both sides, would have prevented a split.

But mutual tolerance was lacking in sufficient strength. Ritual and doctrinal differences were caught up in the more practical and immediate question of Church government and authority. The hierarchs, in their desire to assert their authority, began to demand uniformity with their own usages and their own belief. On the matter of usages it was soon found that there must be some latitude; but on the doctrinal issue Rome brought the matter to a head by inserting the crucial word *Filioque* into the form of Creed that she officially used. This was a challenge that the East could not ignore. It is difficult to take seriously the expressions of horror that Greek theologians were wont to use in expounding the heretical nature of the Roman view; indeed, it is easy for Roman apologists to point out that Greek theology has not in the past been either clear or consistent in its own doctrine about the Procession of the Holy Ghost. But the Eastern Church was genuine in its disapproval of the insertion of a word into the Creed that had been fixed after long and earnest debate and, it was hoped, divine inspiration by the Fathers of the Oecumenical Councils. Whatever opinion the East may have held in the past about the right of the Bishop of Rome to make doctrinal pronouncements, such pronouncements had in the past received endorsement by an Oecumenical Council. Furthermore, the Roman addition of *Filioque* was immediately odious to the Greeks for a purely political reason. It represented the triumph of German influences at Rome. But its more serious aspect was that it raised the whole question of the Pope's right to be the arbiter of Christian doctrine.

In the past the question of doctrinal authority had been less urgent than that of administrative authority. Rome had had a better record for Orthodoxy than any of the other Patriarchates; and the compromise followed at Chalcedon, when Rome stated the true faith, which the council elaborated and endorsed, had hitherto been satisfactory, though the theorists on each side might give it a different interpretation. Far more bitterness had been caused by Rome's claim to interfere in the affairs of the other Patriarchs. The Pope frequently intervened to denounce heresy; but as heresy-hunting was a favourite pastime of most Eastern ecclesiastics, who were often glad to secure Roman support in attacking a fellow, the Pope's intervention was not so angrily resented as was his insistence that the Roman Curia was the supreme ecclesiastical court, to which appeals could be brought from all over Christendom. The Council of Sardica had given this right to Rome. But Sardica was not an Oecumenical Council and when it took place the city of Constantinople had barely been founded and its Patriarchate was not yet established. The Church of Constantinople could soon claim that it had been granted by Oecumenical Councils the same rights and privileges as Rome.

The issue was not clear. It is easy to quote words of Eastern Fathers which seem to admit the full claims of Rome; it is also easy to quote others that deny them. Even the Roman apologists, though they lay more stress upon legal logic and precedent, are not always consistent. Were the Roman claims based on the apostolic succession of the Bishops of Rome from Saint Peter, if, indeed, Saint Peter had been given the exclusive power to bind and to loose, or were they based on the imperial dignity of Rome, the capital of the Oecumene? Or, again, what part was played by the eminence of the Bishops of Rome and their record of unblemished orthodoxy? It seems that the East gave to Rome the primacy and a particular reverence and respect from an imprecise and unanalysed mixture of all these reasons. But one Roman Pope, Anastasius II, was denounced as heretical by his own people, and another, Honorius I, was condemned as a heretic by the universal Church. Meanwhile the foundation of New Rome, which is Constantinople, necessarily detracted from the unique dignity of Old Rome as the Imperial capital. With the Emperor and the Imperial government established in their city, the Constantinopolitans naturally considered that their Church should enjoy equal privileges with those of the deserted capital. They probably felt themselves to be generous in according to Old Rome an honorary primacy; and that they did so was largely due to the weakness of their Church's claim to an apostolic foundation. The rights and wrongs were neither definite nor static; and the course of history added to the confusion.

In the West, when the Roman Empire dissolved before the barbarian invaders, the Roman bishopric survived as the one continuous international institution. But the city of Rome, decaying amongst its vast ruins, was no longer a centre of material political might. In the East Constantinople was steadily growing in wealth and glory; but the power of its Patriarchs was held in check by the presence of the Emperor. Political communications between the two cities never ceased; but cultural connexions diminished. Latin was the international language of Western Christendom and Greek of Eastern; and neither understood the other. Only the bilingual lands of southern Italy served to provide interpreters. There were times when intercourse increased; but these were for the most part times of conflict. When the Iconoclasts dominated Constantinople the opposition there, led by the monks of Studium, insisted on their right to appeal in such a crisis to Rome. The missionary activity of the mid-ninth century and the circumstances of the Patriarchate of Photius led to a series of angry interchanges. But for the most part the Churches of East and West each went their own way, developing their own customs and traditions and avoiding too clear a definition of their mutual relations. Even when there were quarrels and controversy between the hierarchs the congregations were never deeply involved. Saint Constantine-Cyril, the apostle to the Slavs, who was a personal friend of Photius and the leading statesmen of Byzantium, had no hesitation in owning allegiance to Rome when he came to a district where the

Roman connexion seemed to him more practical. Saint Nilus of Calabria clearly felt no barrier between the Churches of Constantinople and Rome. The average Christian in East and West still felt that he belonged to one undivided Church.

It may be that, considering their divergent customs, interests, and ideas, a schism between Eastern and Western Christendom was inevitable. The actual crisis was caused by an extraordinary coincidence of political events in the eleventh and twelfth centuries. The remarkable reform of the Papacy, conducted first by the Western Emperors and then, during the temporary eclipse of the Western Empire, by the Church itself, led to an aggressive and ecclesiastically imperialistic policy on the part of the Popes; and it followed on a period when the Papacy had been decadent and negligible. About the same time there came the Norman invasions of southern Italy, the conquest of a province that was largely Greek by active adventurers belonging to the Latin Church. Byzantium, already in an unhealthy internal condition, had to face as well as the Normans a far more dangerous enemy in the Turks. The Byzantines could not therefore react forcibly enough in Italy. The Papacy could have helped them, but its new policy shocked and irritated them. The Patriarch had already shown his disapproval of German influence at Rome, as exemplified by the insertion of *Filioque* into the Creed, and in protest had refused to include the Pope's name in his diptychs. But, with memories of the recent degradation of the Papacy in their minds it was impossible for the Byzantines to take its new claims seriously. To admit that appeals could be taken from their church-courts to Rome seemed absurd. The Patriarch Eustathius was sufficiently aware of the problems that might arise to suggest a formula defining the position of the sees in a manner that corresponded to actual reality. But the West in its present temper would not agree. At the same time the Emperor needed an ally in Italy against the

Normans; and the Pope was the potentate best suited to help him.

The negotiations of 1054 were an attempt to solve the immediate political problem. That they failed so disastrously was due in the main to the personal characters of the protagonists. Even the intervention of the populace of Constantinople was not based on nationalistic or ideological sentiment but was, rather, a demonstration in favour of a popular Patriarch against an unpopular Emperor and against an alien intruder who had insulted him and the holy shrine of Saint Sophia. The Patriarch's attempt to secure support amongst the Eastern hierarchy in a counter-attack on Rome only met with a limited success. But the episode had increased ill-feeling; and both sides began to formulate their views with a precision that it would have been more tactful to avoid. Differences over the Creed and over usages were underlined; and the situation in southern Italy gave actuality to the problem. Meanwhile against the papal claim to universal supremacy the East set out the theory of the Pentarchy of Patriarchates and the authority of the Oecumenical Councils. The dispute was still between hierarchs and politicians. The congregations were hardly involved, except in southern Italy, where the new Latin masters wished to introduce Latin ways, and, occasionally, in Constantinople when the Emperor answered by closing churches of the Latin rite. But the Papacy began to offend the national sentiment of the Byzantines by excommunicating the Emperor and by encouraging the Normans in their aggression. There were, however, on both sides statesmen and churchmen eager to restore amity. Under Pope Urban II and the Emperor Alexius Comnenus goodwill seemed to have returned.

The Crusades soon followed. Alexius had hoped to use the revived good relations to recruit Western soldiers to fill his depleted armies. Urban, anxious to oblige the Emperor and deeply concerned himself over the advance of

Islam and the difficulties of pilgrimage, and with local western problems to solve, launched the First Crusade, with far greater success than he anticipated. The chief tragedy of the Crusades was that they brought the misunderstanding between Eastern and Western Christians down to a popular level. The Byzantines found the idea of the Holy War incomprehensible and repulsive. They were eager for allies against the Turks but could not interest themselves in wars in Palestine. Meanwhile they resented the large, unruly, and rapacious armies that marched through their lands demanding to be treated as welcome guests. The Crusaders for their part believed that they were coming to rescue Eastern Christendom and were surprised and hurt not to receive a warmer welcome and a fuller co-operation. Soon there was a bitter quarrel between the Emperor and the Crusaders over the city of Antioch and its historic Church, which threw Latin and Greek Christendom into definite opposition. Farther south the establishment of the Frankish Kingdom of Jerusalem and still more its decline caused a cleavage between the Latins and the native Orthodox, whose patron was the Emperor. The Second and Third Crusades increased the antipathy between the ordinary Byzantine citizen and the ordinary soldier and pilgrim in the Holy armies; and this antipathy was encouraged and seemed to be justified by the disputes that continued between the apologists on either side. But at the same time there were throughout the twelfth century political influences that were eager to avoid a breach. The Byzantine Emperor disapproved deeply of the Frankish Prince of Antioch, but he found that the Frankish King of Jerusalem could be of use as an ally. Still more, he needed the political friendship of the Pope for his Italian schemes, to support him against the Normans of Sicily and the Western Empire. His personal influence was continuously used to avert any serious breach.

Contemporary with the Crusades and partly affected by

them was the growth of the commercial power of the Italian maritime republics. The desperate economic position of the Empire had induced the Emperors to give them many trade concessions and privileges in return for immediate naval and financial aid; and the whole international commerce of Byzantium was passing into their hands. The few attempts made by the Imperial government to check them had to be quickly withdrawn. The arrogant prosperity of the Italian merchants was a constant irritation to the Byzantines and added largely to the popular dislike of the Latins. The personal predilections of the Emperor Manuel Comnenus, with his fondness for occidental persons and ways, caused further resentment. Soon after his death it seemed to the Byzantines that their whole government was in Latin hands. They reacted with the massacre of the Latins in Constantinople in 1182, which only served to rouse the anger of the West. All the time churchmen both at Rome and at Constantinople were advertising their differences and thus giving a religious sanction to the increasing mutual bitterness. The weak Emperors of the House of Angelus were powerless to stop the trend towards open hostility, which found its ghastly expression in the Fourth Crusade. The actual course of the Crusade was due more to accident than to deliberate planning; but it cannot be doubted that sooner or later a similar crisis would have been reached. But the horrors of the sack of Constantinople produced an intensity of hatred that could not be forgotten. Though Byzantium was temporarily eliminated and never fully recovered, the Byzantine Church received the strength that always is given by conscious martyrdom. The Pope, caught between his pleasure at the general outcome and his dislike of the methods, missed his one opportunity of recovering goodwill in the East. At the crucial moment he showed himself lacking in sympathy and understanding; and he was never forgiven.

If the schism had arisen merely out of quarrels between

the hierarchs over precedence and customs or even over administrative and doctrinal authority, the sincere attempts made by subsequent Emperors to heal it might have succeeded. But the tragedy of the schism was that it was not a matter of superficial jealousies and conflicting ecclesiastical traditions. It went deeper; it was based on mutual dislike between the peoples of Eastern and Western Christendom, a dislike that arose out of the political events of the eleventh and twelfth centuries. The military aggression of the Normans, the commercial aggression of the Italian maritime cities, and the whole nobly intentioned and savagely executed movement of the Crusades were the causes of the breach, not the petty vituperation of Michael Cerularius and Cardinal Humbert. There had been schisms in the past, but it had been possible to patch them by tact and forbearance, because they had concerned only a superficial section of society. But when the papal demands were backed by the aggressive public opinion of the West insisting on the subjection of the East, and when public opinion in the Orthodox East, remembering the Crusades and the Latin Empire, saw in papal supremacy a savage form of alien domination, then no amount of compromise over the Procession of the Holy Spirit or the bread of the Sacrament would be of avail. The East had no wish to submit to the West and the West would accept nothing less than submission. Even though it seemed later that the only chance of salvation for Byzantium lay in union with the West, the wisest of the later Emperors, Manuel II, sadly warned his son that attempts at union would only worsen the breach; for the Latins were too proud and the Greeks too obstinate to come together again.

The course of political history deepened the schism beyond repair; and beneath the political quarrels there was a profound difference in ideology. The post-Hildebrandine Papacy represented a superb attempt to give the world a new order. The secular powers of the West were local and limited. Even the Western Empire had no oecumenical authority. It was for the Papacy, the one undying institution, with all the prestige of Rome behind it, to provide the control and government that would make of Christendom a Christian unity. It was a magnificent conception; but it was unintelligible to the Christian East. There the secular Empire survived to carry on the prestige of Rome. Caesar was a Christian now, but the things that were his had still to be rendered to him. The complaint of the Byzantine ambassador at Monte Cassino that the Pope had become an Emperor showed the dislike that Byzantium felt for the new Western order. But to the Western thinkers, sure that they had found the way to rebuild society on a steady Christian basis, the refusal of the East to accept the overlordship of the heir of Saint Peter, the Vicar of Christ, seemed wantonly and wickedly obstructive. To the difference in ideology there was added the agelong difference in temperament between Rome and Greece, the former legalistic and authoritarian and the latter philosophical and individualistic. The Churches of Rome and the Orient were prevented by history from keeping to the same path. Their problems were not the same, nor were the answers that they gave to them. That they should maintain unity demanded a breadth of tolerance, of wisdom, and of forbearance that is beyond the reach of most of mankind. Ignorance, folly, and petty jealousy played its part in their separation; but its seeds were sown by forces far removed from their control.

This is not the place to try to assess the consequences of the schism nor to make suggestions how best, after so many centuries, the breach may be healed or narrowed. It would have been pleasant to end this study on a note of hope that, in these dark days, Christendom might somehow close its ranks in perfect unity. But it is too much to expect of any great Church that it should abandon the claims and convictions for which its members have worked and suffered for so long. We can only pray, in all humility, that the followers of Christ should show a warmer fellowship to each other; so that if the Holy Catholic Church cannot march against the enemy as one united army, it can at least march as a company of allies, bound by friendship, respect, and understanding.

BIBLIOGRAPHY

NOTE. The following abbreviations are used in the bibliography and in the footnotes to the text:

Aa.Ss.	*Acta Sanctorum Bollandiana*, Antwerp–Paris–Rome, Brussels, 1643– (in progress).
M.G.H.Ss.	*Monumenta Germaniae Historica, Scriptores*, ed. G. H. Pertz, T. Mommsen, and others. Hanover, 1826– (in progress).
M.P.G.	Migne, J. P., *Patrologiae Cursus Completus, Series Graeco-Latina*, 161 vols. in 166, Paris, 1857–66.
M.P.L.	Migne, J. P., op. cit., *Series Latina*, 221 vols., Paris, 1844–55.
R.H.C.Grecs.	*Recueil des Historiens des Croisades*, Académie des Inscriptions et Belles Lettres, *Historiens Grecs*, 2 vols., Paris, 1875–81.
R.H.C.Lois	Ibid., *Lois*, 2 vols., Paris, 1841–3.
R.H.C.Occ.	Ibid., *Historiens Occidentaux*, 5 vols., Paris, 1844–95.

I. 1. *Collections of Sources*

ALLATIUS, L., *De Ecclesiae Occidentalis et Orientalis Perpetua Consensione*, Cologne, 1648.

BENECHEWITCH, V., *Catalogus Codicum Manuscriptorum Graecorum qui in Monasterio Sanctae Catharinae in Monte Sinai asservantur*, St. Petersburg, 1911.

BEZOBRAZOV, P. V., 'Documents for the History of the Byzantine Empire' (in Russian), *Journal of the Ministry of Public Instruction*, vol. cclxv, St. Petersburg, 1889.

BOHMER, J. F., *Acta Imperii Selecta*, Innsbruck, 1870.

BRIGHTMAN, F. E., *see* Bibliography, II.

CHROUST, A., *Quellen zur Geschichte des Kreuzzuges Kaiser Friedrichs I*, *M.G.H.Ss.*, new series, vol. v, Berlin, 1928.

Collectio Avellana, ed. O. GUNTHER, 2 vols., *Corpus Scriptorum Ecclesiasticorum Latinorum*, No. XXXV, Vienna, 1895.

COTELERIUS, J. B., *Ecclesiae Graecae Monumenta*, 4 vols., Paris, 1677–92.

D'ACHERY, L., *Spicilegium sive Collectio veterum aliquot Scriptorum*, 2nd edition, 3 vols., Paris, 1723.

DE KHITROWO, B., *Itinéraires Russes en Orient*, Société de l'Orient Latin, Série Géographique, No. V, Geneva, 1889.

Demetracopoulos, A., *Bibliothèque Ecclésiastique*, 2 vols., Leipzig, 1866.

Dölger, F., *Regesten der Kaiserurkunden des Oströmischen Reiches*, 3 vols., Munich/Berlin, 1924–32.

Goetz, K., *Kirchenrechtliche und kulturgeschichtliche Denkmäler Altrusslands*, Stuttgart, 1905.

Golubovitch, G., *Biblioteca Bio-bibliografica della Terra Santa e dell' Oriente Francescano*, 5 vols., Florence, 1906–27.

Hagenmeyer, H., *Die Kreuzzugsbriefe aus dem Jahre 1088–1100*, Innsbruck, 1902.

Hefele, C. J., *see* Bibliography II.

Heisenberg, A., *Neue Quellen zur Geschichte des lateinischen Kaisertums*, Munich, 1923.

Hergenröther, J. A. G., *Monumenta Graeca ad Photium ejusque Historiam pertinentia*, Ratisbon, 1869.

Holtzmann, W., *see* Bibliography II.

Jaffe, P., *Monumenta Gregoriana, Bibliotheca Rerum Germanicarum*, vol. ii, Berlin, 1865.

——, *Regesta Pontificum Romanorum*, 2nd edition, ed. W. Wattenbach and others, 2 vols., Leipzig, 1885–8.

Kirch, J. P., *Enchiridion Fontium Historiae Ecclesiasticae Antiquae*, Freiburg-im-Breisgau, 1910.

Leib, B., *Deux Inédits Byzantins sur les azymes au début du XIIe siècle, Orientalia Christiana*, vol. ix, Rome, 1924.

Loparev, C., *Description of some Lives of Greek Saints* (in Russian), *Vizantiiskii Vremennik*, vol. iv, St. Petersburg, 1897.

Mansi, J. D., *Sacrorum Conciliorum Collectio*, 31 vols., Florence/Venice, 1759–98.

Michel, A., *see* Bibliography II.

Patrologia Orientalis, ed. R. Graffin and F. Nau, Paris, 1907– (in progress).

Potthast, A., *Regesta Pontificum Romanorum inde ab anno 1198 ad annum 1304*, 2 vols., Berlin, 1874–5.

Riant, P., *Exuviae Sacrae Constantinopolitanae*, 3 vols. (3rd vol. by F. de Mely), Geneva, 1877–1904.

——, *Inventaire critique des lettres historiques des Croisades*, Paris, 1880.

Röhricht, R., *Regesta Regni Hierosolymitani*, 2 vols., Innsbruck, 1893–1904.

Rozière, E. de, *Cartulaire de l'Église du St. Sépulcre*, Paris, 1849.

Sathas, K. N., *Μεσαιωνικὴ Βιβλιοθήκη, Bibliotheca Graeca Medii Aevi*, 7 vols., Venice/Paris, 1872–9.

SUDENDORF, H., *Registrum oder Merkwürdige Urkunden für die deutsche Geschichte*, 3 vols., Jena-Berlin, 1849–54.

TACCONE GALLUCCI, *Regesti dei Pontifici Romani per le Chiese della Calabria*, Rome, 1902.

THEINER, A., *Monumenta Spectantia ad Unionem Ecclesiarum Graecae et Romanae*, Vienna, 1872.

WATTERICH, J. M., *Pontificum Romanorum qui fuerunt inde ab exeunte Saeculo IX usque ad finem Saeculi XIII Vitae*, 2 vols., Innsbruck, 1880–5.

ZACHARIAE VON LINGENTHAL, *Jus Graeco-Romanum*, 7 pts., Leipzig, 1856–84.

2. *Greek Sources*

Anna Comnena, *Alexiad*, ed. B. Leib, in *Collection Byzantine de l'Association Guillaume Budé*, 3 vols., Paris, 1937–45.

Balsamon, Theodore, Patriarch of Antioch, *Opera*, in *M.P.G.*, vols. cxxxvii–cxxxviii.

Basil I, Emperor, *Epanagoge Basilii, Leonis et Alexandri*, in Zachariae von Lingenthal, *Jus Graeco-Romanum*, pt. iv.

Basil of Caesarea, Saint, *Letters*, in *M.P.G.*, vol. xxxii.

Basil of Ochrida, Archbishop of Thessalonica, *Des Basilius aus Achrida Erzbischofs von Thessalonich bisher unedierte Dialoge*, ed. J. Schmidt, Munich, 1901.

Cedrenus, George, *Synopsis Historiarum*, ed. J. Bekker, 2 vols., Bonn, 1839.

Cerularius, Michael, Patriarch of Constantinople, *Letters*, in *M.P.G.*, vol. cxx; *Synodal Edict*, ibid.; *Adversus Francos* (attributed to Cerularius), in Hergenröther, *Monumenta Graeca ad Photium Pertinentia.*

Cinnamus, John, *Epitome Historiarum*, ed. J. Meineke, Bonn, 1836.

Criminationes adversus Ecclesiam Latinam, in Cotelerius, *Monumenta Ecclesiae Graecae*, vol. iii.

Demetrius Chomateanus, *Letters*, in *M.P.G.*, vol. cxix.

Eustratius of Nicaea, *Orations*, in Demetracopoulos, *Bibliothèque Ecclésiastique*, vol. i.

Greek clergy, letter to Innocent III, see above under *Criminationes.*

John of Kiev, *Canonical Answers to the Monk James*, ed. A. Pavlov, as 'Fragments of the Greek Text of the Metropolitan John's Canonical Answers' (in Russian), *Additions No. 22 to the Publications of the Russian Imperial Academy of Sciences, No. 5*. Also in Goetz, *Kirchenrechtliche und kulturgeschichtliche Denkmäler Altrusslands.*

John the Oxite, Patriarch of Antioch, *Sur les Azymites*, in Leib, *Deux Inédits Byzantins.*

Leo, Archbishop of Ochrida, *Epistola ad Ioannem Episcopum Tranensem*, in *M.P.G.*, vol. cxx.

Leo III, Emperor, *Ecloga Leonis et Constantini*, in Zachariae von Lingenthal, *Jus Graeco-Romanum*, pt. iv.

Mesarites, Nicholas, *Opera*, in Heisenberg, *Neue Quellen zur Geschichte des lateinischen Kaisertums*, vol. i.

Michael of Anchialus, Patriarch of Constantinople, *Dialogue*, given in C. Loparev, 'On the Unionism of the Emperor Manuel Comnenus' (in Russian), *Vizantiiskii Vremennik*, vol. xiv, St. Petersburg, 1917.

Neophytus of Paphos, *De Calamitatibus Cypri*, printed with *Itinerarium Regis Ricardi*. See next section.

Nicetas Chartophylax, *De Schismate Graecorum*, in Michel, *Humbert und Kerullarios*, vol. ii, and in *M.P.G.*, vol. cxx.

Nicetas Choniates Acominatus, *Historia*, ed. I. Bekker, Bonn, 1835.

Nicetas of Maronea, Archbishop of Thessalonica, *Dialogi de Spiritu Sancto*, *M.P.G.*, vol. cxxxix.

Nicholas of Methone, *Βίος Μελετίου τοῦ Νέου*, ed. V. G. Vasilievsky, Publications of the Palestinian-Russian Society (in Russian), vol. vi, pt. 17, St. Petersburg/Jerusalem, 1886.

Peter III, Patriarch of Antioch, *Letters*, *M.P.G.*, vol. cxx; *Systatic Letters*, in Michel, *Humbert und Kerullarios*, vol. ii.

Phocas, John, *A Brief Description*, trans. A. Stewart, Palestine Pilgrims Text Society, vol. v, London, 1896.

Photius, Patriarch of Constantinople, *Letters*, *M.P.G.*, vol. cii.

Phurnes, John, *Ἀντιρρητικὴ Ἀπολογία*, in Demetracopoulos, *Bibliothèque Ecclésiastique*, vol. i.

Prodromus, Theodore, *Poems*, *R.H.C. Grecs*, vol. ii.

Psellus, Michael, *Accusation of Michael Cerularius*, ed. L. Bréhier, 'Un discours inédit de Psellos', *Revue des Études Grecques*, vols. xvi–xvii, Paris, 1903–4; *Funeral Oration on Michael Cerularius* and *Letters*, in Sathas, *Μεσαιωνικὴ Βιβλιοθήκη*, vol. iv.

Stethatus, Nicetas, *Against the Latins*, in Demetracopoulos, *Bibliothèque Ecclésiastique*, vol. i, and in Michel, *Humbert und Kerullarios*, vol. ii. Latin translations in *M.P.L.*, vol. cxliii, and *M.P.G.*, vol. cxx.

Symoen II, Patriarch of Jerusalem, *Sur les Azymites*, in Leib, *Deux Inédits Byzantins*.

Theodore of Studium, *Letters*, *M.P.G.*, vol. xcix.

Theophylact, Archbishop of Bulgaria, *De Iis in quibus Latini Accusantur*, *M.P.G.*, vol. cxxvi.

Theorianus, *Letters*, *M.P.G.*, vol. cxxxiii.

Vita Sancti Nili, *M.P.G.*, vol. cxx.

Zigabenus, Euthymius, *Panoplia*, *M.P.G.*, vol. cxxx.

3. *Latin and other Western Sources*

Aime, *Ystoire de li Normant*, ed. O. Delarc, Rouen, 1892.
Albert of Aix, *Liber Christianae Expeditionis pro Ereptione, Emundatione et Restitutione Sanctae Hierosolymitanae Ecclesiae*, *R.H.C. Occ.*, vol. iv.
Alexander of Hales, *Summa Theologica*, Cologne, 1622.
Alexius I, Comnenus, Emperor, *Letters*, in Hagenmeyer, *Die Kreuzzugsbriefe*, and in Riant, *Inventaire des Lettres historiques des Croisades.*
Ambroise, *L'Estoire de la Guerre Sainte*, ed. G. Paris, Paris, 1897.
'Analista Saxo', *Annales*, *M.G.H.Ss.*, vol. vi.
Anastasius Bibliothecarius, *Acta Concilii Constantinopolitani IV*, in Mansi, *Sacrorum Conciliorum Collectio*, vol. xvi.
Anonymi Gesta Francorum et Aliorum Hierosolimitorum, ed. L. Bréhier (as *Histoire Anonyme de la Première Croisade*), Paris, 1924.
Ansbert, *Historia de Expeditione Friderici Imperatoris*, in Chroust, *Quellen zur Geschichte des Kreuzzuges Kaiser Friedrichs I.*
Anselm, Bishop of Havelberg, *Dialogi*, in d'Archery, *Spicilegium*, vol. i.
Anselm, Saint, Archbishop of Canterbury, *Opera*, *M.P.L.*, vol. clviii.
Assises de Jérusalem, in *R.H.C.Lois.*
Augustine, Saint, *De Fide et Symbolo*, *M.P.L.*, vol. xl; *De Trinitate*, ibid.
Baldwin I, Emperor, *Letter to Innocent III*, *R.H.F.*, vol. xviii.
Barthelemy, *Vita S. Nicolai Peregrini Tranensis*, *Aa.Ss.*, June, vol. i.
Baudri of Dol, *Historiae Jerosolimitanae Libri IV*, *R.H.C.Occ.*, vol. iv.
Benzo of Alba, *Ad Heinricum IV Imperatorem Libri VII*, in *M.G.H.Ss.*, vol. ix.
Berno of Reichenau, *Epistolae*, *M.P.L.*, vol. cxlii.
Bernold of Constance, *Chronicon*, *M.G.H.Ss.*, vol. v.
Boso, *Vita S. Leonis IX* and *Vita Alexandri III*, in *Liber Pontificalis*, vol. ii (see below).
Bruno of Segni, *De Azymis*, *M.P.L.*, vol. clxv; *Vita S. Petri Ananiensis*, *Aa.Ss.*, August, vol. i.
Burchard, *Epistola ad Nicolaum Sigebergensem Abbatem*, in Sudendorf, *Registrum*, vol. ii.
'Chrétiens de Terre Sainte, Lettre à Charles d'Anjou', ed. O. Delaborde, *Revue de l'Orient Latin*, vol. ii, Paris, 1894.
Chronica de Mailros, ed. J. Stevenson, Bannantyne Club, Edinburgh, 1835.
Chronica Minor auctore Minorita Erphordensis, *M.G.H.Ss.*, vol. xxiv.
Chronica S. Petri Erphordensis Moderna, *M.G.H.Ss.*, vol. xxx.
Chrysolanus, Petrus (Grossolano), Archbishop of Milan, *Oratio*, *M.P.G.*, vol. cxxvii.

Conrad III, King of Germany, *Letters*, see below, Wibald.

De la Broquière, Bertrandon, *Le Voyage d'Outremer*, ed. C. Schefer, Paris, 1892.

Dominic, Patriarch of Grado, letter to Peter of Antioch, *M.P.G.*, vol. cxx.

Ekkehard of Aura, *Hierosolymita*, ed. H. Hagenmeyer, Tübingen, 1877.

Ernoul, *Chronique d'Ernoul et de Bernard le Trésorier*, ed. M. L. de Mas Latrie, Paris, 1871.

Eudes of Deuil, *La Croisade de Louis VII*, ed. H. Waquet, Paris, 1949.

Eugenius III, Pope, *Epistolae, M.P.L.*, vol. clxxx.

Frederick I, Emperor, letter to King Henry, in Bohmer, *Acta Imperii Selecta.*

Fulcher of Chartres, *Gesta Francorum Iherusalem Peregrinantium*, ed. H. Hagenmeyer, Heidelberg, 1913.

Gesta Innocentii III, M.P.L., vol. ccxiv.

Glaber, Radulf, *Historia Sui Temporis, M.P.L.*, vol. clxii.

Gregory VII, Pope, letters, in Jaffe, *Monumenta Gregoriana* and *Regesta*, and in Taccone Gallucci, *Regesti.*

Guibert of Nogent, *Historia Hierosolymitana, R.H.C. Occ.*, vol. iv.

Gunther of Pairis, *Historia Constantinopolitana*, in Riant, *Exuviae Sacrae Constantinopolitanae*, vol. i.

Historia Translationis Sancti Mamentis, Aa.Ss., August, vol. iii.

Humbert of Silva Candida, Cardinal, *Bulla excommunicationis Michael, Constantinopolitani* and *Brevis et Succincta Commemoratio, M.P.L.*, vol. clxiii; *Contra Nicetam Stethatum*, ibid., and in Michel, *Humbert und Kerullarios*, vol. ii. See also Leo IX, Pope, below.

Innocent II, letter to the Church of Antioch, in Rozière, *Cartulaire du Saint-Sépulcre.*

Innocent III, *Epistolae, M.P.L.*, vols. ccxiv–ccxvi.

Itinerarium Peregrinorum et Gesta Regis Ricardi, ed. W. Stubbs, Rolls Series, London, 1864.

John of Salisbury, *Historia Pontificalis*, ed. A. Lane-Poole, Oxford, 1927.

Laycus, *Rationes de Sancti Spiritus Processione*, in Michel, *Amalfi und Jerusalem*, see Bibliography II.

Leo I, Pope, *Epistola Dogmatica*, in Hefele–Leclercq, *Histoire des Conciles*, vol. ii. 2.

Leo III, Pope, *Epistolae, M.P.L.*, vol. cxxix.

Leo IX, Pope, *Epistolae, M.P.L.*, vol. cxliii; *Adversus Graecorum Calumnias* (*Dialogus inter Romanum et Constantinopolitanum*)—actually written by Cardinal Humbert—ibid.

Leo of Ostia, *Chronica Monasterii Casinensis, M.G.H.Ss.*, vol. vii.

Liber Pontificalis, ed. L. Duchesne, 2 vols., Paris, 1886–92.

Louis VII, King of France, letters to Suger, *R.H.F.*, vol. xv.
Malaterra, Gaufredus, *Historia Sicula*, *M.P.L.*, vol. cxlix.
Matthew Paris, *Chronica Majora*, ed. H. R. Luard, 7 vols., Rolls Series, London, 1872–83.
Ordericus Vitalis, *Historia Ecclesiastica*, ed. A. Le Prevost, 5 vols., Paris, 1838–55.
Paschal II, Pope, *Epistolae*, *M.P.L.*, vol. clxiii.
Peter Diaconus, *Chronica Monasterii Casinensis*, *M.G.H.Ss.*, vol. vii.
Peter the Venerable, Abbot of Cluny, *Epistolae*, *M.P.L.*, vol. clxxxix.
Princes, Letter of, to Urban II, in Hagenmeyer, *Die Kreuzzugsbriefe*.
Raymond of Aguilers, *Historia Francorum qui ceperunt Jerusalem*, *R.H.C. Occ.*, vol. iii.
Robert of Clary, *La Conquête de Constantinople*, ed. P. Lauer, Paris, 1924.
Robert the Monk, *Historia Hierosolymitana*, *R.H.C.Occ.*, vol. iii.
Sequentia Andegavensis, in Riant, *Exuviae Sacrae Constantinopolitanae*, vol. ii.
Sigebert of Gembloux, *Chronicon*, *M.G.H.Ss.*, vol. vi.
Smaragdus, *Carmina*, *M.P.L.*, vol. cii.
Suger, Abbot of Saint-Denis, *Opera*, ed. A. L. de la Marche, Paris, 1867.
Tractatus Eboracensis, *M.G.H.*, *Libelli de Lite*, vol. iii.
Victor III, Pope, *Epistolae*, *M.P.L.*, vol. cxlix.
Villehardouin, Geoffrey, *La Conquête de Constantinople*, ed. E. Faral, 2 vols., Paris, 1938–9.
Walafrid Strabo, *Liber de Exordiis*, *M.P.L.*, vol. cxiv.
Wibald, *Epistolae Wibaldi*, ed. P. Jaffe, *Bibliotheca Rerum Germanicarum*, vol. i, Berlin, 1864.
Wibert, *Vita S. Leonis IX*, *M.P.L.*, vol. cxliii.
William of Apulia, *Gesta Roberti Wiskardi*, *M.G.H.Ss.*, vol. ix.
William of Malmesbury, *Gesta Regum*, ed. W. Stubbs, 2 vols., London, 1887–9.
William of Nangis, *Gesta Ludovici VII*, *R.H.F.*, vol. xx.
William of Tyre, *Historia Rerum in Partibus Transmarinis Gestarum*, *R.H.C.Occ.*, vol. i.

4. *Eastern Sources other than Greek*

Bar Hebraeus, Gregory Abu'l Faraj, *Chronography*, ed. and trans. E. A. W. Budge, 2 vols., Oxford, 1932.
Beha ed-Din, Ibn Sheddad, *Life of Saladin* (*What befell Sultan Yusuf*), trans. C. R. Conder, Palestine Pilgrims Text Society, vol. xiii, London, 1897.

Daniel the Higumene, *Vie et Pèlerinage*, trans. in B. de Khitrowo, *Itinéraires Russes en Orient*.

Eutychius, Patriarch of Alexandria, *Annales*, trans. E. Pocock, *M.P.G.*, vol. cxi.

Matthew of Edessa, *Chronique*, ed. and trans. E. Dulaurier, Paris, 1858.

Novgorod Chronicle, ed. (in Russian), A. N. Nasomov, Moscow/Leningrad, [illegible]

Vita S. Georgii Hagioritae, ed. and trans. P. Peeters, *Analecta Bollandiana*, vols. xxxvi–xxxvii, Brussels, 1917–19.

Yahya, Ibn Said, of Antioch, *Chronicle*, in *Patrologia Orientalis*, vols. xviii and xxiii, Paris, 1924, 1932.

II. *Modern Works*

K. I. AMANDOS, *Ἱστορία του Βυζαντινοῦ Κράτους*, 2 vols., Athens, 1939–47.

E. AMANN, article 'Michel Cerulaire', in Vacant et Mangenot, *Dictionnaire de Théologie Catholique*, vol. x. See below.

BAYNES, N. H., *The Byzantine Empire*, London, 1925.

BERNHARDI, W. von, *Konrad III*, Leipzig, 1883.

BREHIER, L., *L'Église et l'Orient au Moyen Âge: Les Croisades*, Paris, 1928.

——, *Le Schisme Oriental du XIe siècle*, Paris, 1899.

BRIGHTMAN, F. E., *Liturgies Eastern and Western*, 2 vols., Oxford, 1896.

BUCKLER, G., *Anna Comnena*, Oxford, 1929.

BURY, J. B., *History of the Eastern Roman Empire*, London, 1912.

—— *History of the Later Roman Empire*, 2 vols., London, 1923.

—— *History of the Later Roman Empire from Arcadius to Irene*, 2 vols., London, 1889.

—— *Selected Essays*, Cambridge, 1930.

Byzantium, ed. N. H. Baynes and H. St. L. B. Moss, Oxford, 1948.

CAHEN, C., 'Indigènes et Croisés', *Syria*, vol. xv, Paris, 1934.

—— *La Syrie du Nord à l'Époque des Croisades*, Paris, 1940.

CHALANDON, F., *Histoire de la Domination Normande en Italie et en Sicile*, 2 vols., Paris, 1907.

—— *Les Comnène*. Vol. i, *Essai sur le Règne d'Alexis Ier Comnène*, Paris, 1900; vol. ii, *Jean II Comnène et Manuel Ier Comnène*, Paris, 1912.

COHN, L., Article 'Eustathios, Erzbischof von Thessalonike' in Pauly-Wissowa, *Realencyclopädie der Classischen Altertumswissenschaft*, new edition, vol. xi.

DEMETRACOPOULOS, A. C., *Graecia Orthodoxa*, Leipzig, 1872.
DOSITHEUS, Patriarch of Jerusalem, *Ἱστορία περὶ τῶν ἐν Ἱεροσολύμοις Πατριαρχευσάντων*, Bucharest, 1715.
DUCHESNE, L., *L'Eglise au VIme siècle*, Paris, 1925.
DVORNIK, F., *The Photian Schism*, Cambridge, 1948.
—— *Les Slaves, Byzance et Rome au IXme siècle*, Paris, 1926.
EVERY, G., *The Byzantine Patriarchate*, London, 1947.
—— 'Syrian Christians in Palestine in the Middle Ages', in *Eastern Churches Quarterly*, vol. vi, London, 1945–6.
FLICHE, A. and MARTIN, V., *L'Histoire de l'Église*, 11 vols. published, Paris, 1934– (in progress).
GARDNER, A., *The Lascarids of Nicaea*, London, 1912.
—— *Theodore of Studium*, London, 1905.
GAY, J., *L'Italie Meridionale et l'Empire Byzantine* (867–1071), Paris, 1904.
—— *Les Papes du XIe siècle et la Chrétienté*, Paris, 1926.
GOLUBINSKY, E. E., *History of the Russian Church* (in Russian), 2nd edition, Moscow, 1901.
GRAF, G. 'Die Eucharistielehre der Nestorianers Al-Muhtār Ibn Buṯlān', in *Oriens Christianus*, vol. xxxv, Leipzig, 1938.
GREENSLADE, S. L., *Schism in the Early Church*, London, 1953.
GREGOIRE, H., 'The Byzantine Church', in *Byzantium* (see above).
—— 'The Question of the Diversion of the Fourth Crusade', in *Byzantion*, vol. xv, Boston, 1941.
GRUMEL, V., 'Autour du Voyage de Grossolanus à Constantinople', in *Échos d'Orient*, vol. xxxii, Paris, 1933.
—— 'Le Décret du Synode Photien de 879–880 sur le Symbole de Foi', ibid., vol. xxxvii, Paris, 1938.
—— 'L'Encyclique de Photius aux Orientaux', ibid., vol. xxxiv, Paris, 1935.
—— 'Le Filioque au Concile Photien de 879–880', ibid., vol. xxix, Paris, 1930.
—— 'Jérusalem entre Rome et Byzance: Une Lettre inconnue du Patriarche de Constantinople à son Collègue d'Antioche', ibid., vol. xxxviii, Paris, 1939.
—— 'Les Lettres de Jean VIII pour le Rétablissement de Photius', ibid., vol. xxxix, Paris, 1940.
——, 'La Liquidation de la Querelle Photienne', ibid., vol. xxxiii, Paris, 1934.
—— 'Le Patriarcat d'Antioche', ibid., vol. xxxiii, Paris, 1934.
—— 'Les Patriarches grecs d'Antioche du nom de Jean', ibid., vol. xxxii, Paris, 1933.

Grumel, V., 'La Politique religieuse du Patriarche St. Méthode', ibid., vol. xxxiv, Paris, 1935.

Hefele, C. J., *Histoire des Conciles*, ed. H. Leclercq, 11 vols., Paris, 1907–52. Cited as Hefele–Leclercq.

Heisenberg, A., *Nicolaos Mesarites*, Würzburg, 1907.

Hergenröther, J., *Photius, Patriarch von Constantinopel*, 3 vols., Ratisbon, 1867–9.

Heyd, W., *Histoire du Commerce du Levant au Moyen-Age*, trans. Furcy Raynaud, 2nd reimpression, 2 vols., Leipzig, 1936.

Hill, G., *A History of Cyprus*, 3 vols., Cambridge, 1940–8.

Holtzmann, W., 'Die Unionsverhandlung zwischen Kaiser Alexios I und Papst Urban II im Jahre 1089', in *Byzantinische Zeitschrift*, vol. xxviii, Leipzig, 1928.

Hussey, J. M., *Church and Learning in the Byzantine Empire*, Oxford, 1937.

Jugie, M., *Le Schisme Byzantin*, Paris, 1941.

Krey, A. C., 'A Neglected Passage in the Gesta', in *The Crusades and other Historical Essays presented to D. C. Munro*, New York, 1928.

Krumbacher, K., *Geschichte der byzantinischen Litteratur*, Munich, 1897.

Langford James, R. Ll., *A Dictionary of the Eastern Orthodox Church*, London, 1923.

Leib, B., *Rome, Kiev et Byzance à la Fin du XIe siècle*, Paris, 1924.

Le Quien, M., *Oriens Christianus*, 3 vols., Paris, 1740.

Luchaire, A., *Innocent III: La Question de l'Orient*, Paris, 1911.

Michel, A., *Amalfi und Jerusalem im griechischen Kirchenstreit*, Orientalia Christiana Analecta, No. 121, Rome, 1939.

—— 'Die Botschaft Petros III von Antiocheia an seine Stadt über seine Ernennung', in *Byzantinische Zeitschrift*, vol. xxxviii, Munich, 1938.

—— *Humbert und Kerullarios*, 2 vols., Paderborn, 1924–30.

—— 'Die Römischen Angriffe auf Michael Kerullarios wegen Antiocheia', in *Byzantinische Zeitschrift*, vol. xliv, Munich, 1951.

Miller, W., *The Latins in the Levant*, London, 1908.

Munro, D. C., 'The Speech of Pope Urban II at Clermont', in *American Historical Review*, vol. xi, New York, 1906.

Nau, F., 'Le Croisé lorrain Godefroy de Ascha', in *Journal Asiatique*, series 9, vol. xiv, Paris, 1899.

Norden, W., *Das Papsttum und Byzanz*, Berlin, 1903.

Oster, E., *Anna Comnena*, 3 vols., Rastatt, 1868–71.

Ostrogorsky, G., *Geschichte des byzantinischen Staates*, 2nd edition, Munich, 1952.

OSTROGORSKY, G., *Studien zur Geschichte des byzantinischen Bilderstreites*, Breslau, 1929.

PALMIERI, A., article 'Filioque' in Vacant et Mangenot, *Dictionnaire de Théologie Catholique*, vol. v. See below.

PAVLOV, A., *Critical Essay on the History of Ancient Greco-Russian Polemic against the Latins* (in Russian), St. Petersburg, 1878.

PRAWER, J., 'L'Établissement des coutumes du marché à Saint-Jean d'Acre', in *Revue Historique de Droit Français et Étranger*, series 4, vol. xxix, Paris, 1951.

RUNCIMAN, S., *A History of the Crusades*, 3 vols., Cambridge, 1951–4.

SALAVILLE, S., article 'Jean Xiphilin', in Vacant et Mangenot, *Dictionnaire de Théologie Catholique*, vol. xv.

STADTMÜLLER, G., *Michael Choniates, Metropolit von Athen*, *Orientalia Christiana*, vol. xxxiii. 2, Rome, 1932.

THROOP, P. A., *Criticism of the Crusades*, Amsterdam, 1940.

TOURNEBIZE, H. F., *Histoire politique et religieuse de l'Arménie*, Paris, 1901.

VACANDARD, E., *Vie de Saint Bernard, Abbé de Clairvaux*, 2 vols., Paris, 1895.

VACANT, A., et MANGENOT, E., *Dictionnaire de Théologie Catholique*, 15 vols., Paris, 1899–1950.

VAILHE, S., article 'Constantinople, Église de', in Vacant et Mangenot, *Dictionnaire de Théologie Catholique*, vol. iii.

—— 'L'Érection du Patriarche de Jérusalem en 451', in *Revue de L'Orient Chrétien*, vol. iv, Paris, 1896.

VASILIEV, A. A., *History of the Byzantine Empire*, Madison, 1952.

INDEX

NOTE: *Names of places and peoples which occur frequently in the text, such as Constantinople, Rome, Frenchmen, Italians, or Greeks, are omitted from the index.*